MIGHTY
IS
YOUR
HAND

Rekindling the Inner Fire Devotional Series

REKINDLING
THE INNER FIRE

◆ ◆ ◆ ◆ ◆ ◆ ◆ ◆ ◆ ◆ ◆ ◆ ◆

MIGHTY IS YOUR HAND

◆

*A 40-Day Journey
in the Company of*

ANDREW MURRAY

*Devotional Readings Arranged
and Paraphrased by*

David Hazard
◆

BETHANY HOUSE PUBLISHERS
MINNEAPOLIS, MINNESOTA 55438
A Division of Bethany Fellowship, Inc.

Published by Bethany House Publishers
A Ministry of Bethany Fellowship, Inc.
11300 Hampshire Avenue South
Minneapolis, Minnesota 55438

Printed in the United States of America

Library of Congress Cataloging-in-Publication Data

Murray, Andrew, 1928–1917.
    Mighty is your hand : a 40-day journey in the company of Andrew Murray : devotional readings / arranged by David Hazard.
        p. cm. — (Rekindling the inner fire)

    1. Spiritual life—Christianity. 2. Devotional exercises. I. Hazard, David. II. Title. III. Series.
BV4501.2.M7975   1994
242—dc20   93–50653
ISBN 1–55661–369–5   CIP

*To Gary and Carol Johnson
and
to all the great people at
Bethany House Publishers
who keep "God's light shining
through good books."*

Foreword

O Lord . . . are you not the God who is in heaven?
You rule over all the kingdoms of the nations. Power
and might are in your hand, and no one can
withstand you.

———

2 Chronicles 20:6

If we'd had an angel's-eye view of the
planet during the first half of the 1800s, we would
have witnessed the catch-fire of a great spiritual
reawakening. Blown by the Holy Spirit's breath, it
spread across nations, leaped oceans from
continent to continent. Wherever the fire erupted,
missionaries popped from it like sparks, to carry
the gospel of Jesus Christ out farther into the
surrounding darkness . . . throughout North and
South America, Europe, India and the Far East,
and Africa.

We'd also have watched the darkness try to
dampen and overpower the glories of this Spirit
fire. But that only made it blaze the brighter.

Andrew Murray was one of those who

was pushed to the front lines of spiritual warfare in the great reawakenings a century ago. His 240 spiritual tracts and books, in themselves, had the impact of a spiritual forest fire in millions around the world. Not to mention his "real" work as a missionary pastor to one of the world's largest "congregations," which spread across some 50,000 square miles of wild South Africa and saw tens of thousands led to Christ.

The events of Murray's life are remarkable—but more importantly, Murray knew the real issues in this matter of spiritual warfare. For that reason, his words have been chosen for this volume, seventh in the *Rekindling* series, because they are more like a training manual for strong spiritual warfare than any other collected writings I know.

Through Andrew Murray we get a man's-eye view of this war on God's Light, and that's what we need. We can't predict, control, wrangle, or imitate this fire from heaven, it comes at God's call, sovereignly—though this doesn't seem to stop us from trying to do God's part.

What we can do, what is our part to do, is to learn how men like Murray went about building a holy altar—or more accurately, an anvil—on which his soul could be tempered, struck, and remade in God's fire. More important that we know how to prepare our spirit, so it can be lifted in God's hand and used like a good blade to cut clean.

Today, we are outwardly surrounded by hostile forces in our neighborhoods and school grounds, in the fields of public policy, among friends, family, and co-workers. The mission of Jesus Christ—to win hearts back to God, to set our chained spirits free from sin and self—is hated by an aggressively secular world.

Right here, we run into confusion and double-mindedness. We are called to tear down strongholds—but does God offer us a "battle plan" that will bring a sure win over events and circumstances? We are called to fight the good fight of faith—but why does the front line seem to move? Are we guaranteed to win in the voting booth? In the courts? Over the media? Or do we abandon worldly battlefields and only give first-aid to wounded souls?

We seem to rush into battle—any battle, every battle—without first things first.

The message we get from Murray, like a telegram from the front line, is this: *Fight to bring the rule of God over your own heart—that's the first training needed if you want to survive and win the spiritual war.*

How do we keep alive our own passionate love for God, so our insistence that the world should love Him doesn't sound so hollow? How do we "lead others to Christ" if we keep losing our way in dark unevangelized regions of our own hearts? When the raging lion spirit of the world strikes, how do we dodge his blow with the agility of meekness, obeying the command of the Lamb?

Retaking the strongholds of our own heart—this is where we begin. When the inward look reveals a treasonous affection for the tents and toys of the enemy, that's demoralizing enough. Heap on the painful events of life, and we're too often defeated.

Rescuing us from our *selves*, this is where men like Andrew Murray can help us. From him, we can learn how to win the spiritual war—if we are willing to be changed entirely, our hearts remade on God's fiery anvil. Just as Murray's had to be. . . .

Andrew Murray was born on May 9, 1828, in Graaff-Reinet, a town located on a lush plain 140 miles north of Port Elizabeth, South Africa. His father had emigrated from Scotland to be a missionary pastor, leaving behind a brother, John, who was also a minister. These are the natural circumstances and lineage Andrew was born into: What deeper experiences birthed the spiritual warrior?

Andrew's father took on the duty of training Andrew's spirit and that of Andrew's brother. As they rode together by wagon, or after a day at school lessons, he made it a point to talk with his boys about their spiritual lives, letting them ask questions, pointing out areas where they might be on better guard.

The greatest single impression Andrew's father made on his sons was his prayer for God to come in power. *Revival*. Every Friday evening, he closed himself in his study and cried out: for himself, for South Africa, for the world. *Revival*. The solid wood doors of his study shook with the cries, and so did the hearts of his sons. When the two were sent to Scotland, to be schooled and to live in their uncle's home for ten years, the memory, the word, the prayer never faded. *Revival*.

It seems they got the message: Nothing else in the spiritual life was to be confused with, or accepted as a substitute for the true fire of God. When a spiritual revival began to stir Scotland, the boys were treated to a front-row seat. One of its leaders, William Burnes, brought the revival fire from America, and he became a close friend of their uncle. The young Murrays must have felt the heat a bit uncomfortably when, after one visit, Burnes wrote them this gentle warning: *Don't mistakenly settle for the kind of conversion that allows you to feel comforted because you've escaped judgment and hell—that is weak comfort if it results in something less than actual separation from sins and the rest of the Spirit's real power.*

A good warning, and one they kept in mind when, as young men, both boys decided to prepare for Christian service. When Andrew, at seventeen, began his ministry studies in Utrecht, Holland, he walked onto his spiritual battlefield.

He and his brother found good company among a small group of like-minded students, and good thing, because cold rationalism had deadened many of their teachers, fellow students, and the churches. Christianity had been embalmed in churches that were little more than mausoleums of tradition: the ideas of sin, the need for rebirth, and the hope of knowing Christ personally; all of this was harshly ridiculed—and so was Andrew's group.

In Utrecht, Andrew saw the lines clearly—between what we would call humanist doctrine and what Andrew would see as mere self-exaltation. He stepped over to the Lord's side and declared himself finally converted. The war was engaged.

This early vision—of our need for absolute surrender to Christ, in both our inward and outward life—was the blade-edge that God forged on the sword we know as Andrew Murray. When he took his first Dutch Reformed parish, in South Africa's Transvaal, at twenty-one, he was not fooled by the self-sufficient face of this vast region, known for its "wild dogs and wilder people."

Andrew's vision of the clash between spiritual darkness and Light would lead him to fight numerous front-line battles throughout his life.

On one hand were the lifelong physical challenges of his work. Pleas for young missionary pastors from Europe went mostly unanswered and, as a young man, Andrew covered his parish—50,000 square miles on a dry African plain—on horseback under the hardest weather conditions. Stricken with fevers, he watched traveling companions die from the onslaught. His love and commitment to his people were one secret of his success—and increased his burden. He became so loved by his people that he was chosen to represent the region in South Africa's bid for independence from Britain. Eventually, his wife had to fashion a protective homelife to keep the demands for Andrew and his gifts from crushing him.

Then there was the spiritual war within the Dutch Reformed Church. Its conservatives were entrenched in formalism and tradition; its liberals lobbed bombs at the orthodox views of Jesus, the Bible, and morality, and replaced the gospel with social concerns. This was, in fact, a smoldering conflict in which Andrew would feel the heat.

And then the other hidden warfare—between the Holy Spirit of God and unseen powers—erupted unexpectedly.

In 1860, Andrew was serving a new church in Worcester, a hundred miles east of Cape Town. His father, still pastoring in Port Elizabeth, had been praying for revival for more than thirty years. Andrew's first sermon, on Pentecost Sunday, came from 2 Corinthians 3:8: ". . . will not the ministry of the Spirit be even more glorious?" Odd, that when the Spirit's ministry came, Andrew nearly missed it.

We can see the forces in opposition from the moment the Spirit fell:

An associate was leading a prayer meeting in the sanctuary weeks later. Though the white Christians claimed to oppose racism, the man balked at first when a young black woman stood up in the back of the church and quietly asked if she might pray. All his imprisoning attitudes had to be shaken off before he responded, after a moment, and permitted her to lead a prayer.

Firsthand reports say that the moment she began, a loud noise came from outside the church, like the thundering approach of a freight train. Mouths fell open in fear and amazement . . . and then the noise burst into the sanctuary. Spontaneously, men and women fell to their knees, confessing sins, crying out in repentance. Drawn by the commotion, Andrew was appalled at the disorder and he commanded them to stop this ungodly, dishonoring behavior. They loved their fuming hero, but they utterly ignored him.

Cautious, conservative though he was, Andrew was soon seized by the force of the Holy Spirit.

But in the best sense, Andrew was never swept away by the supernatural fire that fell—not just that once, but more times—and set revival burning throughout South Africa. Neither vivid emotions nor even miraculous healings took the edge off Andrew's first conviction: *that the Holy*

Spirit must give us more inner power to become, like Christ, humble sons and servants, given to the Father's use and disposal, or it is not the truest, purest work of the Spirit at all. There would be powerful signs, but Andrew would never stop holding that line.

In the midst of revival, Andrew was attacked with a lawsuit by liberal church leaders. Since Dutch Reformed was the official state church in South Africa, he'd potentially committed a crime against the nation by teaching doctrines that contradicted modern church dogma—which ran toward heresies such as the teaching that Jesus was not sinless, that there was no literal resurrection, and that souls did exist after death.

Andrew was hauled into endless court debates, defending orthodoxy, which cost him time away from his churches and strained him physically. This debate, plus the false charges that raged against him, were chronicled in the nation's newspapers. This wave of liberalism, however, reached its high water mark. Andrew's defense of biblical Christianity, before the eyes of a nation, won the day.

But for Andrew, the most constant, subtle, deadliest, hardest-won front of spiritual battle would always be the one in his own soul—between flesh and spirit, self and God. There is nothing so clear, in the many hundreds of pages he wrote, as this message: Absolute surrender to God, our loving and holy Father, is the first and last duty of the Christian. Our part is to submit;

God's part is to cleanse, transform, empower, and guide us into good works for His glory.

In regards to good works: Andrew was no pietist, if that meant hiding away from the world in holy little enclaves to "protect" correct doctrine or "holy-living" habits. Churches are not bars, Andrew insisted, where it's enough to throw open the door and the longing for drink draws people in. The poor and lost must be looked up and brought in. "There must be living, loving Christian workers," he said, "who, like Elisha of old, will take the dead into their arms and prayerfully clasp them close until they come to life again." Wherever he went, he was the first to invade poor areas and black townships to found Sunday schools and promote better education.

And in regards to the inner life: Andrew would only grow stronger in his writing, preaching, and reaching for an inner life that is separated from the world for God's sole use. "It will not do to press too much on the one side of holiness and communion with Jesus, without the other side of the work," he said. "There is . . . no communion closer than 'Go into all the world and teach—and lo! I am with you.' And yet the joy of work and revival is not enough. "God's children must be led into the secret of the possibility of unbroken communion with Jesus personally."

Till the end of his days, in January 1917, this was more than his message; it was Andrew Murray's life.

In compiling *Mighty Is Your Hand*, I have Bethany House Publishers to thank specially because most of the entries are drawn from Bethany's editions of Murray's works, and titles following the entries refer to those books. As always, the prayers are my own, suggested in response to the Scriptures and Murray's words.

For those who feel the urgency, the call to spiritual warfare, I can recommend no more reliable lieutenant than Andrew Murray. His life and his words reveal, more than anything else, that he trained himself in loyalty and obedience to Jesus Christ, the captain of our salvation—and for that reason, his words have both a painful and pleasing way of cutting deep into the soul, like a fine two-edged sword (see Hebrews 2:10; 4:12).

Murray's life tells us that God does this mightiest, cleanest, brightest, best "warfare" with well-made swords.

May this book rekindle in you a desire to become a holy weapon, purified and made strong in the Spirit's fire, perfect—not in ourselves—but because we are fitted to the hand of the Father. May these words offer you training and encouragement in the holy warfare, for our souls and the souls of the world, to which we are called.

David Hazard
December 1993

Contents

MIGHTY
IS
YOUR
HAND

1
Safe Shelter, Mighty Refuge

In you, O Lord, I have taken refuge . . .
be my rock [and my] strong fortress to save me. . . .
Into your hands I commit my spirit. . . .
In the shelter of your presence you hide [me] . . .
in your dwelling you keep [me] safe. . . .
Praise be to the Lord, for he showed his
wonderful love to me.

Psalm 31:1–2, 5, 20, 21

Taste and see that the Lord is good; blessed is the
man who takes refuge in him . . . those who fear . . .
[and] seek the Lord lack no good thing.

Psalm 34:8–10

In many places, Scripture speaks of fear as something wrong and sinful and, in the strongest terms, forbids us to fear. The words "fear not" occur in nearly one hundred places.

Yet in many other places, another kind of fear is praised as one of the true expressions of godliness. The people of God are referred to as "those that fear the Lord." This type of *godly fear* is "acceptable to the Lord," and, if we fear in this way, we will see fruitful blessing in our lives.

The simple distinction between sinful and godly fear lies in this fact: One is fleshly and unbelieving—while the other is believing and full of faith.

A sinful, and very harmful, type of fear flows out of a heart that lacks trust in God. This kind of fear comes out of us when we have a carnal desire to please man—that is, when our greatest fear is to lose the respect and approval of others. If that is our heart's disposition we will fail to say, or to act on, what is right and just and true. This kind of fear also flows out of the heart that has fixed its sense of well-being on the temporal world—on homes, possessions, money, and people. This is the kind of fear that stands condemned.

The true fear of the Lord, on the other hand, flows from the heart that is learning to rest itself in complete trust in God. It stands firmly and waits in hope for God. This type of fear is absolutely indispensable for the spiritual life. So it is no wonder that Scripture commands us to grow in childlike confidence and love for God, for this type of trust honors the Father.

What we are talking about, then, is the absolute assurance that a child has in a good father—and for the Christian, this means we may live freely as children, having a confidence that is deeply rooted in respect for the character and the word of the Father. It is not at all like slavish, cringing fear. It is the simple *belief* that God governs every aspect of our lives in goodness and love, and so we fear to trust in anything else.

This is where we must begin then, with a godly fear of the Lord, and now I hope that you understand why the Scriptures proclaim this as the source of all blessing and power.

The one who fears the Lord in this way—with a quiet, confident assurance that God can never fail, no matter what the circumstances may look like—this man or woman will fear nothing else in this life.

The godly fear of the Lord *is* the beginning of all wisdom. And we may say, too, that the fear of the Lord is the sure way to enter into God's protection and His favor. . . .

THE BELIEVER'S NEW LIFE

My Father, *I believe that, by your all-powerful hand, worlds and universes were formed . . . that you are mighty beyond all imagination . . . that all my strength, obedience, and allegiance is due you.*

And yet my inner vision of your power becomes so

darkened when my eyes are fixed on things of this world . . . on threatening circumstances . . . on challenging people . . . on my own failures and lack.

Help me to begin, today, a new journey in faith. Lift my sight above this world, and lead me inside the mighty fortress of your light and love and goodness . . . until I fear nothing in this life because I am confident in you . . . and only you.

2

Water of Life

There is a river whose streams make glad
the city of God, the holy place
where the Most High dwells. . . . The Lord Almighty
is with us; the God of Jacob
is our fortress.

Psalm 46:4, 7

Jesus said, "Whoever believes in me, as the Scripture
has said, streams of living water will flow
from within him."

John 7:38

God is an ever-flowing spring of the purest love and of blessedness.

Christ is the reservoir, and in Him the fullness of all that God is was collected in human form so that grace could be made visible to us—and in Christ, God's grace is now fully opened to us.

The Holy Spirit is the stream of living water that pours out from under the throne of God and of the Lamb.

The Redeemed—that is, we who are God's believing children—are the spiritual "watercourses" through which the love of the Father, the grace of Christ, and the powerful working of the Holy Spirit are brought to earth and spread to other men and women.

What a clear picture we get here of the wonderful partnership in which God includes us as dispensers of the grace of God! If we understand this illustration, it will help us to learn something, by comparison, about prayer, which is the means by which we bring ourselves into contact with the spiritual stream of *life* offered to us in God.

When we pray mostly for our own needs, this is only the very beginning of the life of prayer. There is a greater glory we can seek in prayer. And that is, we can experience power as intercessors.

To be an intercessor is to bring the grace of Christ and the might of the Holy Spirit upon those souls which are still in darkness.

The more closely the channel is connected to the reservoir, the more certainly will the water flow unhindered through it. The more we are caught up in our prayers with the fullness of Christ and the Spirit who proceeds from Him, and the more firmly we abide in fellowship with Him, the more surely will our lives be happy and strong.

And even this is only a preparation for the

reality. The more we give ourselves over to fellowship, the more we converse with God—the Father, Son, and Spirit—the sooner we will receive the courage and ability to pray down blessing on souls, on ministers, and on the Church around us.

Are you truly a "watercourse" that is always open, so that spiritual life may flow through you to thirsty ones in a dry land? Have you offered yourself without reservation to God, to become a bearer of the energizing operations of the Holy Spirit? Or is it, rather, that you have experienced very little of the power of prayer because you have thought only of yourself when you pray?

You must understand this: The new prayer life into which you have entered in the Lord Jesus can only be sustained and strengthened by intercession, in which you labor for the souls around you, to bring them to know the Lord.

Meditate on this—God *is* a wellspring of love and blessedness that flows without ceasing. And I, as His child, am a living channel through which every day the Spirit of life can be brought to the earth.

THE BELIEVER'S PRAYER LIFE

My Father, I have been living on the dry crusts of my own judgments and opinions. I have fed myself on your Word. And still I have wondered why sometimes my prayers bring little life to others or to me.

Now, in this moment . . . I ask that you wash through me with your Holy Spirit . . . to cleanse my heart and mind of angry, small, and corrupted thoughts toward others. Renew me within, in the wellspring of your unending love.

3
Right in Heart

"The most important [commandment]," answered Jesus, "is this: '. . . Love the Lord your God with all your heart and with all your soul and with all your mind and with all your strength.' "

Mark 12:29–30

May [God] strengthen you with power through his Spirit in your inner being . . . that you, being rooted and established in love, may have power. . . .

Ephesians 3:16–18

Our place of spiritual refuge is this—complete faith in the Lord's goodness and His fearsome might. Therefore, we must begin to see how this kind of simple faith causes us to live. Though we might say many things about the life of faith, the principal attitudes that will spring from our hearts are these:

We will have a holy reverence and awe as we come

in praise, worship, and prayer before the glorious majesty of God, the all-holy One. This attitude of respect will guard our hearts from the superficiality that forgets who God is, so that we treat Him as somehow equal to us—demanding of Him, speaking to Him any way we like. It will guard us from thinking we can live with little concern for sinful habits, so that we fail to honor God with our daily lives.

Our hearts will be filled with humility. By that I mean, we will learn to be fearful of our own human strengths and abilities—coupling that distrust of self with total confidence in God. Once we are awakened to the subtlety of our own hearts—how often we *say* we are relying on God, when really we are trying to control everything ourselves—it is then we will have a holy fear of doing anything contrary to the will or honor of God.

Why will we have this dread? Because we will see how often we lie to ourselves and to God— *saying* that we are obeying God's will, when we are really working hard and manipulating circumstances in order to gain the desires of our own will.

One who abandons his natural strengths in order to depend fully on God for protection is humble indeed. And this same humility will fill him with love and gentleness in everything he says and does, toward everyone he meets.

Thirdly, *we will live in an attitude of cautious*

vigilance over our souls. I do not mean the type of unhealthy scrutiny that endlessly looks for wrong motives in ourselves. I mean that we will set apart time to give holy forethought to our plans, seeking God to show us the right path. When we do this, He helps us to keep watch against the enemy. He will help guard us from making important decisions too hastily, and from saying or doing something in a thoughtless manner that we will greatly regret later.

Finally, *we will have a holy enthusiasm and courage*—a heart that is always alert for chances to advance the kingdom of God. Though evil circumstances may oppose us, though our own flesh begs us to leave our spiritual post, when we hold fast to this attitude—with the faithfulness of a true servant—we will not give up on even the smallest duty, no matter how thankless or seemingly insignificant it may appear.

And so I say again, the heart that surrounds and safeguards itself with these attitudes—this is the heart that will remain strong in the face of all puny, worldly fears. From this heart will flow inconceivable courage in the face of danger, sickness, betrayal, or opposition. Why? Because this heart is at rest in the might of the Lord, and that can only mean certain victory in the end.

THE BELIEVER'S NEW LIFE

My Father, lead me inside the walls of your love and goodness . . . where I am safe to trust you . . . knowing I am hidden with Jesus in you.

In this secret place with you . . . purify me in your tempering fire . . . let your words form the new clean edge on my soul . . . and make me keen to serve only you . . .

So that I will faithfully stand against all darkness, in your love and beautiful Light . . . no matter how hard the wind blows against me.

4
The Perfect Path to God

For who is God besides the Lord?
And who is the Rock except our God?
It is God who arms me with strength
and makes my way perfect.

Psalm 18:31–32

Jesus said, "Be perfect . . . as your
heavenly Father is perfect."

Matthew 5:48

To be *perfect* before God is not only the calling and the privilege of "great" men of faith— as we think of men like Abraham—it is equally the calling of all God's children.

The call to "be perfect" comes to each one of us: No one who claims to be a Christian may avoid it, or refuse to obey it, without endangering his salvation.

In great measure, though, we misunderstand what it means to be perfect. It is not a command like "You shall not kill" or "You shall not steal." These commands are given in reference to a limited sphere of our life—that is, the outward, physical realm. "Be perfect" is an inner, spiritual principle that lies at the very root and determines whether or not our religion is false or true.

What does it mean, then, to be perfect?

If our service to God is to be acceptable, it must not be with a divided heart but with a heart that is whole toward God.

Many are prevented from keeping this command, and that is chiefly because we misunderstand what religion is. It is this: Man was created simply to live for God, to show forth His glory—and we do that by allowing God to show how completely He can reveal His spiritual likeness and blessedness in us.

Do you see it? God lives for man, longing in His great love to communicate His goodness and love. It was to restore this life, lost by sin, that Christ came to redeem us—to bring us back (See Colossians 1). In selfishness, we look upon salvation merely as the escape from hell. And in this same selfish way, we want only so much of holiness as is needful to make our personal safety, comfort, and happiness secure.

Jesus Christ came meaning for us to be restored to the state from which we had fallen. Salvation, then, is the state in which the whole inner man—the heart, the will, the life—is given up to the glory and service of God. . . . The enthusiastic devotion of the complete inner man is what is asked of us. . . .

THE BELIEVER'S SECRET OF A PERFECT HEART

My Father, I am so thankful that Jesus, your Son, shed His blood to bring me into your kingdom of light . . . to bring me home to you!

Come into my soul today, by your Holy Spirit, and shed more light. Show me where I betray you for the sake of my own comfort.

5
The Battleground

*For in my inner being I delight in God's law; but I
see another law at work in the members of my body,
waging war against the law of my mind. . . . The
mind of sinful man is death, but the mind controlled
by the Spirit is life and peace . . . [and] those who are
led by the Spirit of God are sons of God.*

Romans 7:22–23; 8:6, 14

*Your word is a lamp to my feet and a light for my
path. I have taken an oath and confirmed it, that I will
follow your righteous laws.*

Psalm 119:105–106

God's highest glory is His holiness. Because
this virtue of holiness is a true vein that makes up
His very nature, He can do nothing other than to
hate and destroy evil. He does so, not to harm
us, but because He wants to lead us into a life of
freedom—for by nature He also loves and works
for our good.

In man, it is *conscience* that cooperates in the good, freeing work of God by condemning what is sin and by approving what is right. Conscience is the remains of God's image in man, the nearest thing to any part of the divine. It is conscience in us that guards God's honor amidst all the ruin of the Fall. Consequently, as God begins His work of redemption—that is, bringing us out of our pitiful captivity to darkness and death into His light and life—He will begin by renewing our conscience.

The Spirit of God is the Spirit of His holiness. We must see conscience as a spark of divine holiness. It is the essential work of the Holy Spirit, as He works to renew us and set us apart for God's purpose, to bring harmony between our innermost thoughts and desires and our outward words and actions. It is also His most intimate work in us, revealing all that darkness has concealed.

The believer who would be filled with the Holy Spirit, who wants to experience God's blessings in the fullest, must give rightful place and honor to his conscience. When we become faithful to our conscience—not silencing it when it pricks us, not excusing ourselves as "too weak to obey," but heeding its inner warnings—we make our first steps in the path to being restored to the holiness God offers. To be intensely honest with ourselves as the searchlight of conscience reaches our innermost self, open to His loving light which sets us free—this is both a groundwork and a characteristic of spirituality that is "perfect" and true.

It is the work of conscience, aided and enlightened by the Holy Spirit, to show us how to make a correct response toward everyday duties of service and friendship, and toward God. And it is also the work of conscience to assure us that God accepts our faith in Christ and our acts of obedience. So, as the Christian life progresses, we can expect that these works of conscience—our inner conviction and God's voice of conviction in us—these two will become increasingly identical.

Soon, we will feel the need to say—and a great freeing happiness comes when we *can* say—along with Paul: ". . . my conscience confirms it in the Holy Spirit" (Romans 9:1).

Conscience can be compared to the window of a room through which the light of heaven shines. Through this window, our soul can look up into heaven—into the freedom and joy of living in the presence of God. And by the light of heaven we can see, more clearly each day, all that God's light shines upon within our heart. Our heart is the room in which every aspect of our true life dwells—that is, our ego, or soul, with all its powers and affections.

On the walls of our heart, the laws of God are written. Even in the one who is a total unbeliever, even in a heathen, these laws are still partly legible, though sadly darkened and defaced. In the believer, the law is written anew by the Holy Spirit in letters of light. At first, these letters glow dimly—but they grow clearer and brighter as they are exposed to the light of heaven, flowing into the room from without. And this is where our duty lies: to freely, willingly open ourselves to the light of heaven, which is nothing less than the powerful action of the Holy Spirit, wanting to penetrate our innermost being, where Light can meet light.

Do you see how urgent it is that we open ourselves to this light? That we cooperate with its work in us?

For with every sin I commit, the light of God will shine in upon it: first, to expose both the motive and action and show it for the deadly sin it is; and second, to show me how such an act only brings death to my soul, to show me that it is therefore a crime against the life within me— and so it stands condemned.

If the sin is not confessed and forsaken, then I have chosen to smear the window into my soul with a stain. The stain remains, blocking the Light. Therefore, my conscience has become defiled because my mind refused the good teaching of the Light (see Titus 1:15). If we are not vigilant, the window to our soul is smeared with one sin after another, growing darker and darker until the Light can hardly shine through at all.

It is no wonder, then, that we as Christians can sin and not feel the slightest disturbance or remorse: It is the result of blotting out the light of conscience, so that we are in darkness and numb to all healthy sense of conviction.

The Holy Spirit's first action is to cleanse and restore what sin has defiled within us. By restoring conscience to full and healthy action, He helps us to experience the wonderful, empowering grace of Christ. . . . In this way, He empowers the believer to live in the full light of God's favor.

The window of the heart that looks heavenward *is* cleansed by the Holy Spirit—and must be *kept* clean by our cooperation with His work—so that we can walk in the light.

THE SPIRIT OF CHRIST

My Father—Father of Lights! I thank you that you have not abandoned me to outer darkness. I thank you that you ignite my conscience . . .

About my unforgiveness toward another . . . about "shaping" facts to suit my purposes . . . about times when I excuse myself but hold others up to a harder standard. . . .

Continue your good, good work today . . . restoring your Lighted pathway for my soul.

6
Growing

Jesus said, "This is what the kingdom of God is like.
A man scatters seed on the ground. Night and day,
whether he sleeps or gets up, the seed sprouts and
grows, though he does not know how. All by itself the
soil produces grain—first the stalk, then the head,
then the full kernel. . . ."

Mark 4:26–28

[Jesus] is the Head of his body, the church . . . and
each part in its own special way helps the other parts,
so that the whole body is healthy and growing and full
of love.

Ephesians 4:15–16, TLB

Life is always movement, change, progressiveness. Increase and growth is the law of all created life.

Consequently, the new *spiritual life* in us is also destined to increase—and it can only increase by becoming stronger.

In any seed, and in the earth, there is a type of life and a power to cause growth. When these two meet, the seed is impelled by its very nature to begin growing until it reaches its full height and bears fruit. In the same way, the seed of eternal life is planted in the soil of our souls, and this seed wants to increase and grow with a divine growth, until we become "perfect"—and that means we are destined to grow more into the image and likeness of Christ, with the complete humility, trust, obedience, and spiritual power that were the fruit of His life.

In a parable about seeds, Jesus teaches us two of the most important lessons on the growth of the spiritual life.

. . . The truth is, all we can do is to let the life of the Spirit grow within us. *We can do nothing to force ourselves to grow in spirit.*

It is from within that the power of spiritual life must come—in order to be true spiritual growth, and not self-righteous striving, our growth must come from within, from the Life and the Spirit planted in us. We do not hold the power to create new spiritual life, and so we can contribute nothing to this side of it. *It shall be given to us to grow.*

For as Scripture declares, God is the one who will create in us true spiritual growth (Isaiah 61:3). All that we can do is to let the life grow.

On the other hand, all that *hinders* the Life from growing in us we must take away and keep away. That is our part. If there are thorns and thistles that fill up the place in the soil which the plant must have, we can see to it that those useless, fruitless, evil things are removed. In order to grow strong the "plant" must have its place in the soil, and the soil cannot be shared with evil weeds.

This is our work, then, as gardeners. As we clear our lives to make a place for the spiritual life to grow, the Spirit will grow within us of himself.

This is the understanding you must have when you hear it said that "you must surrender your heart entirely and not hold back a single part for any other purpose" in order for the new spiritual life to grow in you. It means that you must hold watch over the motives, plans, and thoughts of your heart, the way a gardener jealously watches over his land so that nothing but the chosen crop can take possession and fill it. It means that we surrender our being, so that the one good crop—the Spirit of Christ—may grow free and unhindered in us.

The wise gardener knows what he must provide for the crop in the way of nourishment and water, replenishing the soil's nutrients and moistening the ground as needed. So we must see that our spirit is nourished out of the Word, and that in prayer we receive the living water of the Spirit. . . .

But we must also understand that all growth is gradual. . . . Do not expect everything at once.

Give God time. . . . It is by abiding in the earth that the plant grows. It is by standing continuously in grace—standing in Christ, in whom God has planted us—that the new spiritual life will grow.

Slowly but surely . . . this divine growth will produce in our lives a "perfect" crop—that is, the living image of Christ.

THE BELIEVER'S NEW LIFE

My Father, I am so grateful that you are kind and patient. I want to make my inner being a place that is set apart for you.

Come in your Spirit, Lord. I open my soul to the work of your hand, so that you can produce in me good growth . . . a crop of gentleness . . . goodness . . . self-control . . . the image of your Son in me.

7
Founded on Goodness

The Lord is good to those whose hope is in him, to the one who seeks him.

Lamentations 3:25

"There is none good, but God."

"His goodness is in the heavens."

"How great is your goodness, which you have stored up for them that fear you."

"O taste and see that the Lord is good."

The foundation of our spiritual life rests upon knowing that, as Scripture repeats, the God we serve is a good God—that everything He plans and says and does has at its root the motive of goodness. But how do we enter into His goodness and experience it in our lives, so that our hearts overflow with constant rejoicing— how, I ask, when we are surrounded by so much that is bad?

The *way* we enter into God's goodness is made

clear by the prophet Jeremiah in his *Lamentations*. We must learn how to place all our hope in God—which is to say, we learn how to *wait* upon Him to reveal His goodness in due time.

The Lord is good. But His own children often do not know that He is good as a matter of absolute fact, and that is because we do not learn how to quiet our soul so that God can reveal to us that He is always and only good.

Do you want to fully know the goodness of God? Then give yourself more than ever to a life of waiting on Him, of resting all your hope in Him.

As we first learn to wait on God our hearts are chiefly set on all the blessings we are hoping for, and an easy life. God graciously uses our simple needs to train us and prepare us for something much higher than we were thinking of. We were seeking gifts: He, the giver, longs to give us *himself.*

And so it is often for this very reason that He withholds the gifts we are asking for; it is for this reason that the time of waiting is so long. Only as we rest in God himself, who *is* goodness, can our soul even begin to find its satisfaction.

THE BELIEVER'S SECRET OF WAITING ON GOD

My Father, *are there circumstances in my life that have caused me to accuse you of being unfair? Caused me to question your goodness?*

Open my eyes, Father, to the standard of fairness
and goodness that I have set—and then used to
measure you by. Help me to see, with eyes of deeper
faith, that this is backwards—that you are Goodness
itself . . . that living close to you . . . living in your
Spirit . . . is the standard against which all the other
events of my life must be measured.

8

Before God's Throne

Walk in the Spirit, and ye shall not fulfill the lust of the flesh. . . . And they that are Christ's have crucified the flesh with the affections and lusts. If we live in the Spirit, let us also walk in the Spirit.

Galatians 5:16, 24–25, KJV

*I*n the midst of his teaching about "walking in the Spirit," Paul tells us the only way by which deliverance from the fleshly sinful nature is to be found. Those who walk in the Spirit "have crucified" the sinful nature.

When we understand what it means to crucify the sinful nature—when we *experience* what it means to do so—then we will know what it means to "walk in the Spirit." Anyone who longs for the freedom that comes from walking in the Spirit must first grasp what Paul is saying.

The "flesh"—in Scripture, this expression means every bit of our human nature in its fallen condition, under the power of sin—it includes our whole being—spirit, soul, and body. After the Fall, God said, "Man is flesh" (Genesis 6:3), meaning that all man's power, intellect, emotions, and will had fallen under the power of the flesh. Scripture tells us . . . that in our flesh no good thing dwells (Romans 7:18).

So it is that our minds, when they lie under the power of the flesh, are at enmity with God (Romans 8:7). So nothing that the fleshly mind, or will, thinks or does can have any value in the sight of God—no matter how good a show we make, no matter how much we may glory in our "brilliant" plans and accomplishments. In fact, the great danger in our religion—the cause of its weakness and failure—is that we have confidence in the fleshly mind, with its worldly wisdom and its works.

In order to be pleasing to God, the self-will and self-effort of our flesh must be entirely given up. We must do so in order to make way for the willing and working of another—and that is the Spirit of God. . . .

So then, what does it mean to "crucify the flesh"?

Some Christians are content merely to accept Paul's statement as a general, doctrinal truth: The cross takes away the curse, which was upon flesh. Some others think they must inflict pain and suffering on their flesh—to deny it or mortify it. Still others think only of the moral influence the cross will exercise, seeing it as a symbol of Christ's great sacrifice. And each of these views holds an element of truth.

But if we are to understand the real *spiritual significance* of what Paul means, we must go to the root of his thought: To crucify the flesh is to give it over to the curse. The cross and the curse are inseparable (Deuteronomy 21:23).

To say "I have been crucified with Christ" means something very serious and awe-inspiring. It means that I have seen that my old nature, my *self*, deserves the curse—and there is no way to get rid of this *self* accept by death. It means that I voluntarily give this *self* over to death.

And at the same moment, it means that I have accepted as my new life the Christ who came to give himself—His own flesh—to the cursed death of the cross. I accept into myself the life of the One who received His new life because He accepted death. And this means I accept as my new mode of living the same virtue of *willing submission to God, no matter what is required of me*, which was the attitude and mind of Christ (Philippians 2:5–8).

Following the example of Christ, then, I must give my old man, my *self*, with its will and work, as a sinful, cursed thing, to the cross. It is nailed there—and in Christ I am dead to this old self.

And free from it.

. . . If I only know the cross as the place and moment where Christ substituted himself for me, if I never understand the cross as the means whereby I enter into spiritual fellowship with Christ in His Spirit, then I will never know its power to set me apart from the sinful nature.

As the blessed truth of this fellowship dawns, I see how by faith I enter into spiritual communion with Jesus. I see how I can live in spirit with Jesus who, as my head and leader, proved that the cross is the only "ladder" by which I ascend to God and stand before His throne.

THE SPIRIT OF CHRIST

My Father, you have been so kind in sending Jesus to show me how I can come alive in your Spirit. I have used my own "strengths" to live by for so long . . . used the force of my will to achieve . . . my words and actions to change and manipulate circumstances.

Please, my Father . . . help me to let go of these sickly strengths, which demonstrate how small is my faith in you. I will take on the childlike trust and obedience of Christ as my true strength.

9
The Spirit of Truth

Jesus said, "When the Counselor comes, whom
I will send to you from the Father . . . he will testify
about me. . . . But when he, the Spirit of Truth,
comes, he will guide you into all truth. He will not
speak on his own; he will only speak
what he hears. . . ."

John 15:26; 16:13

*I*n promising the Holy Spirit to His disciples,
our Lord speaks of Him as the Spirit of
Truth. . . .

As He teaches and guides us into the Truth,
the Spirit—which is Christ—does not give us
only words, thoughts, and images from
without—that is, from a book or a teacher. He
teaches by entering the secret roots of our life,
where He plants the truth of God as a seed. And
then He dwells there in us, with the power of
divine life, waiting for us to cooperate in the
seed's growth.

How do we do this? We cooperate by faith, by

waiting on God in joyous expectation, and by surrendering our will and goals to Him—and in this way we cherish and nourish the hidden life of the Spirit in us. Then the Lord, who dwells in Spirit within us, may quicken and strengthen His seed of spiritual Truth, causing it to grow strong and spread its branches throughout our whole being, until it produces spiritual fruit where it may be seen—that is, in our words and actions.

Therefore, we must see that the Spirit reveals Christ and all He has for us, not from without but from within, not in word but in power. It is the Spirit who makes Christ—who has been to us so often only an image, a thought, a Savior outside and above us—to be Truth within us. . . .

There are Christians who are afraid that if we think too much of the Spirit's presence within us we will be led away from honoring, respecting, and having a godly fear of the Savior as He lives and reigns in majesty above us. It is true that, if we only look within ourselves, we may indeed take our eyes off of Christ. But we may be sure that the silent, believing, adoring recognition of the Spirit of Truth will not allow us to slip into such an error.

No, fixing the eyes of our inner man upon Christ—upon the truth and grace and life which He brought from heaven as a spiritual reality to communicate to us—this will only lead us to a more true and spiritual apprehension that Christ alone is, indeed, all in all.

The Spirit of Truth is the one who reveals to our inmost being—that deepest place inside, from which all of our attitudes, thoughts, words, and actions proceed—the knowledge that Christ in us *is* life and truth. He causes us to experience His power from within, the power with which He works and saves. . . .

And the mark of this Spirit of Truth is a wondrous, divine teachableness . . . that gentle teachableness which marks the poor in spirit, the broken in heart. This is seen in the men and women who have become conscious that, just as their own righteousness is worthless before God, so their own wisdom and power for apprehending spiritual truth is just as worthless. . . .

May the Spirit of Truth open our eyes to the reason why so much Bible reading, Bible knowledge, and Bible preaching produces so little fruit of holiness in the lives of believers. Too often, the Bible is studied and held in fleshly minds, with wisdom that is not inspired from above—that is, a wisdom that was asked for and waited for from God. The mark of the Spirit of Truth was wanting.

The Spirit of Truth speaks not from himself, nor from His own perceptions. He speaks only what He hears. The Spirit of Truth receives everything day by day, step by step, from God in heaven. He is silent and does not speak, except and until He hears.

THE SPIRIT OF CHRIST

My Father, the approach of your holy light feels fearsome . . . and burning. . . .

And then I know you have come only to burn away the bonds of sin . . . my dependence on the world, my own flesh, and other people . . . so that I am free to rise and walk in your Spirit.

Come, Spirit, in your burning holy power, into my inmost being. In this moment, burn away my bonds!

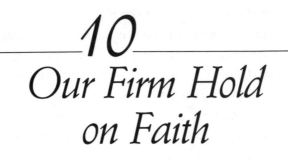

10
Our Firm Hold on Faith

Keep hold of the deep truths of the faith with a clear conscience.

1 Timothy 3:9

Maintaining a good conscience toward God from day to day is essential to the inner life of faith. Each one of us may make a clean conscience our aim, and accept nothing less. . . .

The more we seek the testimony of a clean conscience—that we are doing what is well pleasing to God—the more we will feel the freedom, every time we are overtaken with a failure, to look at once to the blood of Jesus, which continues to cleanse us. . . .

For many of us, the weakness of our faith comes from the lack of a clean conscience. Notice very carefully how Paul links these two, as he instructs Timothy to "hold on to faith and a good conscience, for some have rejected these and so have shipwrecked their faith" (1 Timothy 1:19).

Conscience is the seat of faith. If you want to grow strong in your faith and have boldness with God, you must first know that you are pleasing Him (1 John 3:21–22). Jesus said most distinctly that it is for those who love Him and keep His commandments that the promise of the Spirit is meant—the promise that the Father and the Son will come to make their home within us. . . .

How can we live this kind of wonderful life—at peace with God because we have a clean and free conscience?

The first step is to humble yourself under the reproofs of your conscience. Don't be content with the kind of general confession that sounds humble—"Oh, yes, I know I'm a sinner and there are so many things wrong with me." That is not the real thing. And beware, on the other hand, of allowing yourself to fall into the trap of the painful, scrupulous conscience that mistakes temptation for real sin.

No, if we are going to die to the flesh and the rule of sin by the power of the indwelling Spirit as Paul promises (See Romans 8:13), we must deal with the *practice* of sin. . . .

Accept anew Christ's wonderful offer to take entire possession of your heart, to dwell in you as Lord and keeper. Trust Him to do this by the power of His Holy Spirit—even and *especially* when you feel most weak and helpless.

Remember that obedience—that is, taking

Christ's words into your will, so that you may keep them in your actual life—this is the only way to prove the reality of your surrender to Him. . . .

Vow in faith that, by God's grace, you will seek to grow in the blessing of a conscience that is clean toward both God and man.

THE SPIRIT OF CHRIST

My Father, I am only fooling myself when I try to "hide" sin from you. At best, I only push it around behind me, where I no longer see it . . . and where it grows in heaps, and spills across the floor of my soul.

Today, Father, turn my head to look at the one sin on which I trip again and again . . . because I have refused to see it until now.

11
Chief of Sinners

*Here is a trustworthy saying that deserves full
acceptance: Christ Jesus came into the world to save
sinners—of whom I am the worst.*

1 Timothy 1:15

I fear that there are many Christians who use
strong expressions of self-condemnation and self-
denunciation in seeking to humble themselves.
And yet the genuinely humble spirit—the "heart
of humility," which is accompanied by kindness,
compassion, meekness, and forbearance—this
spirit is still as far off as ever.

Being occupied with *self*, even if it comes in
the form of deep self-hatred, can never free us
from self. Only when God opens our spiritual
eyes to the whole truth will we bow in deepest
humility of spirit—that is, when we see that God
has both condemned our sin by His law, *and* that
He delivers us from sin by His grace.

For the law may only break the heart with
fear. Only grace works in us sweet humility, the

core of our new nature, which becomes a fountain of joy to water the soul.

It was the revelation of God—so high and holy yet drawing close to make himself known in beauty and grace—that made men of faith such as Abraham and Jacob, Job and Isaiah, bow so low.

In your own soul, learn to see that God the Creator is *all* to the creature in its nothingness. See that God the Redeemer, in His grace, is *all* to the sinner in his helplessness. The soul that waits for and trusts and worships this God will find itself so full of His presence that there will be no place for self. Only in this way can the promise be fulfilled: "The arrogance of man will be brought low and the pride of men humbled; the Lord alone will be exalted in that day" (Isaiah 2:17).

When, as sinful men and women, we dwell in the full light of God's holy, redeeming love— when we experience that full indwelling of divine love which comes through Christ and the Holy Spirit—who cannot but be humble?

It is not in being occupied with sins, but in being occupied with God, that we will experience blessed deliverance from self.

HUMILITY

My Father, walk closely with me . . . be strong in me . . . so that I may see the truth and not lie to myself.

When I wring and twist inside, thinking that others treat me as inferior, isn't there a deeper truth that I have not admitted? . . . That I want to see myself as better than I am, deserving better treatment than I am given?

Isn't it true that I often refuse to see my old self as condemned . . . and that the only way out of my self-centered heart is the path that leads me through your forgiveness?

12
God, Our Source

The Lord upholds all those who fall and lifts up all who are bowed down.

Psalm 145:14

*P*salm 145 is a psalm of the kingdom . . . and points specifically to the needs of God's saints—especially those who fall and are bowed down.

And after this promise of the Lord's unfailing love, we read: "The eyes of all look to you, and you *give* them . . ." (v. 15). That is, nothing is nobler or more blessed in the exercise of our free will than to use it in waiting on God.

Sometimes an army is sent out to march into an enemy's country. And sometimes the news is received back at home that the army is not advancing. At once we want to know the cause of their delay. Very often the answer comes back: Waiting for supplies. If the stores of food, clothing, and ammunition have not arrived, they cannot dare to advance.

It is no different in the Christian life, as it

must be lived out in the real world, which is the enemy's camp: Day by day, for every step, we need our supplies from above. It is absolutely necessary to cultivate a spirit of dependence on God, and confidence in Him, refusing to go on without the needed supply of grace and strength for the battle.

Unfortunately for us, there can be a lot of praying . . . and very little waiting on God. Why? Because when we pray we are often occupied with ourselves, with our own needs, and with our own efforts in presenting those needs to God—thinking that if we find just the right way to present our needs, then we can make God hear and answer.

But when we wait on God, our first thought is of the God on whom we wait. We enter His presence. And immediately we feel we need simply to be quiet so that He, as God, can overshadow us with himself. Waiting on God gives Him time, in His own way and divine power, to come to us. . . .

Before you pray. . . .

Bow quietly before God.

Remember who He is, how near He is, how certainly He can and will help.

Be still before Him, and allow Him to stir up in your soul the childlike disposition of absolute dependence and confident expectation.

Wait on God, I say, as a living being—as the living God who notices you and is longing to fill your every need. Wait on God until you know you have met Him.

Pray in this way, and prayer will become so different.

And when you are praying, let there be intervals of silence—reverent stillness in your soul—in which you yield yourself to God in case He may have something He wishes to teach you or to work in you.

Waiting on Him will become the most blessed part of prayer, and the answer to your prayer will be twice as wonderful because it is the fruit of your fellowship with the Holy One.

WAITING ON GOD

My Father, you are so mighty that you can lift my inmost being . . . when my ego has been singed and I'm fragile as burned paper . . . when sin has snapped my spirit like a broken reed . . . when I need your hand to help me rise again, and experience tells me I've turned from you too many times.

Today, Father, I place myself in your strong hands again, trusting you to restore my soul in confidence that you will never leave me . . . that you will complete your work in me.

13
The Ways of God

*Show me your ways, O Lord, teach me your paths;
guide me in your truth and teach me, for you are God
my Savior, and my hope is in you all day long.*

Psalm 25:4–5

I spoke about an army that entered into an
enemy's territory but had to wait for supplies
before advancing. This army could also have sent
home the message "Waiting for orders and
instructions."

If an army has not received the latest, up-to-
the-minute instructions from its commander-in-
chief, then it does not dare to make a move.

Again, it is the same in the Christian life: We
not only have a deep need to wait for supplies—
we have just as deep a need to wait for
instructions from our Commander!

Look how beautifully this comes out in Psalm
25. If we read the entire psalm, we learn that the
writer knew and loved God's law supremely, and
meditated in that law day and night. But he knew

this was not enough. He knew that in order to grasp the truth in the right way, in order to apply it to his life in a way that was right for his specific circumstances, then he needed direct teaching from God.

This psalm is peculiar because the author repeatedly confesses his need for divine teaching, and also because he repeatedly shows his childlike confidence that the proper instruction will come. Study this psalm, and your heart will be filled with two thoughts—first, that you have an absolute need for God's guidance and, second, that if you seek Him you will certainly find it!

The Father in heaven is so interested in us, His children. And He longs so much to keep our lives in step with His will and His love. Therefore, He is willing to keep our guidance entirely in His own hands, knowing so well that we do not do what is really holy and heavenly unless He works it in us. And He intends His own demands to become promises of what He will do in watching over us and leading us all day long.

We can count on God, then, to teach us His way and show us His path, not only in special trials and hard times but in everyday life.

What is needed in us to receive this guidance?

We must become fully conscious of our ignorance about what God's way may be, fully conscious of our need to have God's light shine within us, showing us the way, until our way becomes brightly lit as a path at high noon.

Finally, wait quietly before God until you are filled with a restful assurance. It will be given for "He guides the humble in what is right and teaches them in his way" (v. 9). . . .

What we need in order to live a life that is guided by God is very simple: We must only believe that God is the *only* source of wisdom and goodness, and that He longs to be to us all that we could possibly need.

Waiting on God

My Father, you are all-wise . . . and in your wisdom you guide me on paths that are always good.

I need your guidance today—you are my only hope! Even though I may be deaf to your voice, blind to the way I should go, that doesn't hinder you.

Open my ears . . . heal my eyes.

14
Holiness That Shines

*As far as God is concerned there is a sweet,
wholesome fragrance in our lives. It is the fragrance of
Christ within us . . . to those who know Christ
we are a life-giving perfume.*

2 Corinthians 2:15–16, TLB

When we speak of the current "holiness movement," we praise God for it. We hear a great deal about those who are seeking after holiness, about those who profess to be living holy lives, about holiness teachings and meetings. The blessed truths about holiness in Christ and holiness by faith are being emphasized as never before.

The great test of whether the holiness we claim to seek and attain is *truth* and *life*, however, will be this: It will produce in our lives increased humility.

The one thing that is absolutely necessary, in

order for God's holiness to dwell in the creature—
a holy beauty that *shines* through us—is humility.
In Jesus, the Holy One of God who makes us
holy, a divine humility was the secret of His life
and His death and His exaltation. Likewise, the
one infallible test of our holiness—that is, our
willingness to rest under the hand of God—will
be the humility before God and men that marks
us.

Humility is like a brilliant bloom, which gives
to the world the fragrance of Christ, showing that
a life is truly rooted in God's holiness.

The chief mark of counterfeit holiness is its
lack of humility. Everyone who seeks after
holiness needs to be on guard, for it is all too
easy to slip into our own self-efforts, trying to
finish God's work with our fleshly efforts, even
after we have experienced what it means to walk
in the Spirit (See Galatians 3:1–3). Pride is so
deadly, and it creeps in at the moment it is least
expected.

Pride can lift its head in the very temple of
God and make even the worship of God the
scene of its own exaltation. . . . And the moment
when we would stand before men to confess our
deep sinfulness is the very moment when we
must be on watch over our souls. . . . For on the
day when the sons of God came to present
themselves before Him, Satan was also among
them (See Job 1:6). . . .

Remember this: In our spiritual lives, you and

I may have had certain times when we were broken and humbled, but this is not the same thing as being clothed with humility. We must clothe ourselves every day, every moment, in every situation, with a humble spirit, having a lowliness of mind that counts itself the servant of others, demonstrating in word and action the attitude that was in Christ Jesus (See Philippians 2). . . .

Jesus, the Holy One, was the humble one: The holiest will always be the humblest. There is none holy but God: We have as much of holiness as we have of God. And the measure we have of God will be the measure of our real humility.

For humility is nothing but the disappearance of self in the vision that God is all.

HUMILITY

Holy Father . . . in this moment, quiet my heart.

Help me to look beyond my own poor attempts at righteousness . . . to understand the beauty of your holy humility . . . as you come to walk with me . . . to live in me.

15
Praise That Lasts

Jesus said, "How can you believe if you accept praise from one another, yet make no effort to obtain the praise that comes from the only God?"

John 5:44

We know of Christians who have blessed experiences, or they are so gifted in ministry they bring powerful blessings to others . . . and yet they are lacking in humility. I'm sure that you are inclined to wonder about this. Don't these people prove that they have a true, strong faith, even though they seek too much the honor that comes from men?

There is more than one answer that can be given to this situation, for these are not simple matters. But the principal answer is this: These people indeed have a measure of faith, and in proportion to their faith special gifts are bestowed upon them, and in proportion to this measure of faith they are able to bring spiritual blessings to others. But in that very same blessing, the work of their faith is hindered through the lack of humility. Therefore, the blessing they bring is often superficial and does not last because they are not the *nothing* that opens the way for God to be *all*. A deeper humility would without doubt bring a fuller blessing.

I tell you, the Holy Spirit must be allowed to work in us, not only as a Spirit of power but infusing our souls, our thoughts, and our actions with the seasoning of compassionate grace toward others. Then He will communicate through us, not just in words, but in lives of much power, holiness, and steadfastness in God. Such lives are, sadly, too seldom seen. . . .

Brothers and sisters in Christ, nothing can cure you of the desire to receive respect from men but to give yourself over to seeking only the honor that comes from God. Likewise, continuing to honor the glory that comes from God is the only thing that can cure you of the sensitivity and pain and anger that come when the respect of men is not given!

Let the glory that will come to you from the all-glorious God be everything to you. You will be freed from the glory of men and of self, and be content and glad to be nothing. Out of this spiritual nothingness, you will grow strong in the true faith, which is faith in God alone. . . .

You will find that the deeper you sink in humility before God, the nearer He draws to you. And when He dwells so near, in the very center

of your soul, you will find that He is able to fulfill
every desire of your faith.

*F*ather of Glory, I know it's true . . .
that the praise and honor that comes from men feeds
something in me.

Today, I declare a "fast" on seeking glory from
others. Help me, Father, in my weakness, to come into
the secret place with you . . . to hear your simple
instructions . . . to obey without the need for anyone
else to know . . . to rest in the confidence that you see.

The glory be to you alone, Master!

16
Seeing God

No one has ever seen God; but if we love each other,
God lives in us and his love is made complete in us.
We know that we live in him and he in us, because he
has given us of his Spirit.

1 John 4:12–13

"No one has ever seen God. . . ." It is true
we may not yet have the ability to see God
himself with our eyes. The all-consuming, all-
absorbing fire of God's glory—a fire and glory so
great it brings dissolution to all that is of our
present nature—cannot come into contact with
our fallen earthly state.

But there is given to us a type of "sight" that
is equal to physical vision, and it is given in order
to prepare us and train us for the heavenly vision
we will enjoy one day. The spiritual sight I am
talking about will also satisfy the soul by allowing
us to "see" all that we can contain of God in our
present state.

No, we cannot see God—but can have God

himself living and dwelling within us. We can "see" Him as His love completes our faith. Though we may not see the burning brightness of God's glory we *can* know, in the depths of our being, what is the very essence of that glory— God's love.

God's love perfects and completes our faith. As we become channels that God's love may flow through, God himself comes more clearly in view, abiding within us. This is the heaven we can have on earth. How do we enter into this blessed state? God dwells in us, and His love completes us, if we love one another.

We may not see God—but we do see the men and women and children with whom we live every day. And in them, we have objects that repay us for the lack of our ability to see God. They are given in order to awaken and call forth God's love within us. They are given, as gifts of God, in order to exercise and strengthen and develop that love. By their loving actions as well as their offenses, they will draw the love of God down from its place in the heavenly realm so that it comes to take up its home within us—if we will only let it.

In my brother, I have a tangible created being. And as I live with this one, God tells me to test and try and prove all my love to him. In loving him, no matter how unlovable he may be . . . we allow the flame of holy fire—the flame that consumed the sacrificial Lamb of God—to consume our *self*.

This, then, is how God's love becomes perfected, or completed, in us. In this way it becomes truth, that God himself is living and loving others from within us.

THE BELIEVER'S SECRET OF A PERFECT HEART

Loving Father, I want to keep myself within your love . . . allow your love to burn in me and warm others with its many flames . . . with the warmth of patience, kindness, gentleness, meekness. . . .

There is one who always causes me to react in anger . . . or envy . . . when what they need is your brightness. Today, Father, fill me where I am deficient in your love.

17
Hunger

*My heart and my flesh cry out
for the living God.*

Psalm 84:2

*T*he way we live has a great influence on the
way we pray. . . .

We need to recognize this as spiritual fact:
Man's entire life is a continuous "prayer" to
nature, or to the world. That is, we look at our
needs and immediately look out at the world,
fixing our desire on created things in nature,
hoping they will satisfy our needs.

This natural prayer, or desire, in us can be so
strong (even in men and women who also pray to
God) that the words of prayer we utter cannot be
heard. Have you ever considered that, at times,
God cannot hear the prayer of your *lips*, because
the worldly desires of your *heart* cry out to Him
so strongly and so loud?

. . . A worldly life, and a self-seeking life,
makes prayer powerless. It makes an answer

impossible. With so many of us, there is a conflict between the life and the prayer, and unfortunately the life holds the upper hand.

But the reverse can also be true. Prayer can exercise a mighty influence over our life. I can give myself completely to God when I am in prayer—trusting Him to show me my truest needs, and waiting in hope with the certainty that He will answer in His way in His time. Then prayer can conquer the life of the flesh and sin. Do you see it? Your entire life, and mine, can be brought under the powerful inner direction of God with this kind of prayer. . . .

A word of caution. Because of a defective spiritual life, many people think that they must work themselves up into "spiritual fervency" or emotion in order to pray more. They don't understand that the spiritual life must be strengthened first—which means growing in the deepest trust and love for God, so that we become more and more willing to rest in whatever His will and direction may be. As our spirit becomes stronger in this type of inner life, our prayer life will grow stronger, too.

. . . My prayer must rule my whole life. What I request from God in prayer is not decided in the words I say to Him in five or ten minutes. . . . What I desire from God must really fill my heart the whole day.

It is then that the way opens for the prayer to be answered—and it is then that an answer is sure.

THE BELIEVER'S LIFE OF PRAYER

My Father, *what is it that I desire, more than I desire you? What is it that will cause me to turn away from you if it is taken, or denied me?*

I acknowledge you now, as Sovereign Lord, of all that I mistakenly possess as mine. May your will be done . . . and help me to be at one with your will.

18
Abrasives

I, [Wisdom], was appointed from eternity, from the beginning, before the world began. . . . Blessed is the man who listens to me, watching daily at my doors, waiting at my doorway. . . .

. . . rebuke a wise man and he will love you.

Proverbs 8:23, 34; 9:8

Look upon every man, woman, or child who tries your patience or angers you as a means of grace to humble you. Use every opportunity to humble yourself before others as a means of help, sent directly from God, to keep you living in peaceful submissiveness before Him.

God will accept this humbling of yourself as the proof that your whole heart desires to be purified by Him. Telling God that you receive even the most irritating things as coming from His hand, to sift your heart of self-will, is the very best prayer you can offer.

More than that, learning this foundational lesson—of peaceful rest in God, no matter the painful circumstances—is your preparation for the mighty work of grace that God wants to do in you. And the great work will take place when, by the power and strength of the Holy Spirit, the Father holds the very center of your being in the palm of His hand, and then He will be able to reveal Christ fully in you.

God himself, in His form as a servant, will be truly formed in you and will dwell in your heart.

This is the perfect spiritual path, the living Way of Christ, that leads to the death of our old sinful nature and to the experience of resurrected life in Christ. . . .

Beware of the mistake so many make. They insist that they want to be humble—but they are afraid to be "too humble." They have so many qualifications and limitations, so many reasonings and questionings as to what true humility is and what it is intended to do. They never fully yield themselves to it.

Be sure of this one thing: At the root of all your growth in grace, and of all true advancement in your separation unto God, and of all your increasing conformity to the likeness of Jesus, there must be a deadness to self that proves itself to God and to men in your attitudes and behavior, especially at the moment when someone has been abrasive. . . .

If we say that we have received into our hearts Jesus, the Lamb of God, it means two things— meekness and death. Let us pray and seek, and

be sure to receive Him in both forms. In Christ
Jesus they are inseparable: They must be
inseparable in us, too.

*My Father, I have seen things in such
a wrong light.*

*When I have been misunderstood . . . ignored . . .
corrected . . . insulted . . . confronted . . . something
in me rises up to defend. I churn inside, waiting for a
chance to blame . . . to counterattack.*

*But today I want to be more like Jesus, the Lamb. I
place myself under your all-powerful hand. Help me to
receive all correction as from you . . . to bear all
misunderstanding in your strength.*

19
Spirit of Prayer

*The Lord, who stretches out the heavens, who lays
the foundation of the earth, and who forms the spirit
of man within him, declares,
". . . I will pour out
. . . a spirit of grace and supplication. . . ."*

Zechariah 12:1, 10

*T*he Holy Spirit is "the spirit of prayer."

Twice in Paul's letters there is a remarkable
reference to Him in the matter of prayer:

"For you did not receive a spirit that makes
you a slave again to fear, but you received the
Spirit of sonship. And by him we cry, '*Abba*,
Father' " (Romans 8:15).

"Because you are sons, God sent the Spirit of
his Son into our hearts, the Spirit who calls out,
'*Abba*, Father' " (Galatians 4:6).

. . . The Holy Spirit is given for the express
purpose of teaching us, right from the very
beginning of our Christian life, to utter that word
in childlike trust and surrender. . . . What a

wonderful proof that God has done His utmost to make prayer as natural and effectual as the cry of a child to an earthly father!

It is a sad proof that the Holy Spirit is a stranger to many of our churches when prayer is regarded as a *task*, or even a *burden*. It shows that we do not recognize that God himself has already poured out the Spirit, so that His voice will resonate within our own simple childlike heart-cries—and all the while we look upon prayer as something burdensome and unnatural!

Does this not teach us something about our prayerlessness? It says to me that we must seek for the deeper root of prayerlessness in our *ignorance* about the Divine Instructor whom the Father has sent to teach us how to pray. . . .

Our first work in learning how to pray is this: We must come simply into God's presence—not with our ignorant, pleading prayers, not with our many words and thoughts, as if we must convince God to do what we want, but in childlike confidence that the very work of God is being carried on in us by the Holy Spirit. This kind of confidence will help us to rest in reverent joy and quietness of soul. When we are so at peace in His mighty presence—like a child resting every weight of concern in the arms of its father, depending on the help the Holy Spirit gives—then it will be a matter of great joy to lay our desires and heart-needs before God. . . .

Let us firmly believe, as a divine reality, that

the Spirit of God's Son—the Holy Spirit—is in us. . . . We should fix our souls on this fact: Our inmost heart is His temple, and He dwells within us to bring the full rule of God to the farthest corner of our souls and, consequently, to every action and word in the daily lives we live out among men. . . .

Many Christians pray for more of the Spirit, and this is right—*if* alongside that prayer we recognize the truth that the Spirit wants more of *me*. Just as my soul has possession of my whole body for its dwelling place—that is, it has my whole body at its service—so the Holy Spirit wants to have my whole being as His dwelling place, entirely under His control. No one can continue for very long in prayer, or with much true zeal, without seeing that the Holy Spirit is gently leading to a place where we so trust Him from the depths of our being that our whole lives—body, soul, and spirit—are set into His strong and loving hands, for His use.

"Blessed are they who . . . seek [the Lord] with all their heart" (Psalm 119:2). If we learn how to rightly rest in the Holy Spirit, to pray in childlike confidence, then this declaration will become our life's motto.

THE BELIEVER'S PRAYER LIFE

*F*ather of my spirit, I often forget
myself and try to tell you how to manage affairs . . .
becoming stiff and inflexible . . . or driving.

Teach me how to pray as a child, live as a child . . .
how to trust you today for each weighty matter, each
unyielding person . . . everything that lies beyond my
power to manage.

20
Jesus, the Promiser

*Jesus said, "I tell you, whatever you ask for in prayer,
believe that you have received it, and it
will be yours."*

Mark 11:24

*T*he promise of answer to prayer is one of the
most wonderful in all of Scripture. Yet in the
heart of many Christians it raises the question:
"How can I ever have the kind of faith that *knows*
it will receive all it asks?"

When the Lord gave that promise to His
disciples, He preceded it by telling them where
faith for answered prayer rises from: "Have faith
in God" (v. 22). . . .

The power to believe a promise depends
entirely on faith in the promiser. If you trust in a
person, then you will trust in his word. It is only
when we live and trust in God in a loving
relationship that we will grow in the ability to
believe that He gives when we ask. By that I
mean the sort of relationship in which we have

learned that we can open our whole heart to God, so that our inmost being is continually opened to the mighty influences of His holy presence within.

This connection between faith in God and faith in His promise will become clear if we think what faith really is. . . .

Faith is the ear by which I hear what is promised, and the eye by which I see what is offered—and more importantly, I see *who* is making the offer. The power to take into my hands something that is promised depends first on these other abilities. I must hear the person who makes the promise—because his very tone of voice gives me courage and assurance to believe. And I must see him—because the light in his eye and the welcoming look on his face will make all hesitancy, fear, or suspicion in my heart evaporate.

Do you see it? The value of the promise does not depend on us and our ability to trump up faith on our own—it depends on us seeing, with the unclouded eyes of faith, the *Promiser*. When I know the true, good, and loving nature of the Promiser, then I will have faith in what He promises.

That is why Jesus said, when He made the wonderful promise about prayer, "Have faith in God." That is: Let your eye be opened to gaze upon the living God, and dwell on all that He is by nature—beautiful in holiness, a fountain of goodness, unfailing in love. In this way, we see Him who is invisible. . . .

Believing in God is to open my soul to receive into my soul His love, which overshadows the lives of all who have hidden themselves with Christ in Him. . . . Through the eye of faith, the Light of God's presence streams into my soul, so that I am not in darkness as to all His mighty workings in me and around me.

The soul is created so that the thing I most behold is the thing that lives in me. And so it is in this way—by faith—that God lives in me.

THE SECRET OF BELIEVING PRAYER

My Father, overshadow me with your brightness . . . with the light of promise that I am alive in you.

Show me how I have shaped my heart around some matter, some person I have prayed for . . . trying to press and conform it to my dark understanding. I let go of it now.

Help me to believe, really, in you.

21
Prayer and Fasting

The disciples came to Jesus privately and said, "Why could we not cast
[the demon out of the little boy]?"
. . . Jesus said to them,
"Because of your unbelief. . . .
This kind does not go out except by
prayer and fasting."

Matthew 17:19–21, NKJV

When the disciples saw Jesus cast the evil spirit out of the boy who was having violent seizures—a boy they had been unable to cure— they wanted the Master to tell them the cause of their failure. After all, He had given them power and authority over all devils and all diseases. They had already used this authority on many occasions, and they exuberantly reported how the demons were subject to them.

Yet this time they had utterly failed and wanted to know why.

First, we must understand that there was

nothing in the will of God that made deliverance impossible, nothing in the nature of the boy to prevent it—and we know this because, at Christ's bidding, the evil spirit had been cast out. . . . The Master proceeded to tell them that this kind of spirit could not be driven out, except by fasting and prayer.

See this: Faith is the simplest exercise of the spiritual life, and it is also the highest. Of course I am referring to the kind of faith where my spirit yields itself in perfect receptivity to God's Spirit, and by doing so it is strengthened to its highest ability to act upon God's directives.

This is the point where faith depends upon the kind of spiritual life we maintain. Only when this kind of faith is strong and in full health—that is, when the Spirit of God has full sway in my life—is there the power of faith to perform mighty deeds. . . .

Jesus says to His disciples, in other words, it is not possible to overcome such stubborn resistance as you witnessed in this evil spirit, unless you have the faith that comes from living very close to God and you have found out how to separate yourselves in spirit from the world and the flesh. We learn to live close to God, and we learn how to separate ourselves from the powers of this world, when we understand the true purpose of fasting and prayer.

In this one instance, Jesus teaches us two lessons about prayer. . . .

First, we need a life of prayer in order for faith to achieve its full growth. . . . If we want to know where and how our faith is to grow, the Master points us to the throne of God. In prayer, we enter by faith into secret fellowship with God. When the eyes of our faith behold Him as Creator and Lord of all, we grow in the other kind of faith that is seen as God's power is made manifest in this world.

Faith can only live by feeding itself on what is divine—by "feeding," as it were, on God himself.

I am speaking here about learning to adore God, which is true worship. In prayer, we learn to steer the soul into a deep silence. And there, we let go of ourselves into His care, His guidance, His lordship. In this manner, we grow in the ability to know and to trust God.

In this place of spiritual stillness, we take His words from the Blessed Book, and bring them to Him. We ask Him to speak the Word to us in His own living voice. And the power comes, fully, to believe and receive the Word as God's very own . . . spoken to us!

To prayer we must add fasting in order for faith to grow to its fullest extent.

Prayer is the one hand with which we grasp the invisible. Fasting is the other hand, with which we let loose and cast away the visible world.

There is little that connects us more closely to the world than our need for food and our enjoyment of it. . . . There may come times of intense desire when you become aware that the body, with its appetites, hinders the spirit in its battle with the powers of darkness. At that moment, you may feel the need to keep the body in subjection to the spirit. . . .

Fasting helps to express, to deepen, and to confirm the resolution that we are ready to sacrifice anything—even our selves—in order to gain what we seek for the kingdom of God.

God himself accepted and rewarded the fasting and sacrifice of Jesus the Son. And He will reward you and me with spiritual power when we are ready to give up all for Christ and the sake of His kingdom.

THE SECRET OF BELIEVING PRAYER

Father, I am facing situations far beyond my power to change or influence. Help me to give up my viewpoint, and to see your viewpoint. . . . Show me what this situation is meant to accomplish in your kingdom.

Make me hungry for your will to be done, so that I stand firm in faith . . . rejoicing to see your answer . . . whether it comes late or soon.

22
Pardoning Grace

*Jesus said, "And when you stand praying,
if you hold anything against anyone,
forgive him, so that your Father in heaven
may forgive you your sins."*

Mark 11:25

*E*very prayer depends upon our faith in God's pardoning grace. So many are blocked in prayer on this point that it is important for you to see your way through clearly.

If God dealt with us according to our sins, not one prayer could be heard. Pardon opens the door to all God's love and blessing. And because God has pardoned all our sin, our prayer can prevail, and we can receive all that we need.

The solid, sure ground on which we can stand, on which we can know that we will have answer to prayer is nothing else but the bedrock of God's forgiving love. When assurance of God's love for us has so taken possession of the heart, then we pray in faith. And, conversely, when we are unshakable in our knowledge that God loves us, we begin to live in love toward others.

God's forgiving disposition, revealed in His sacrificial love for us, becomes our disposition. This forgiving love is a mighty spiritual power, and when it is shed abroad in our hearts, when it takes over our entire inner being, then we can freely forgive as He forgives.

If a terrible, painful injury is done to us, or if we suffer injustice, the first thing we must do is to lay hold of a God-like disposition. This is the only way to keep our spirit from latching on to a sense of wounded honor. If we allow the wound to fester, then we will begin down the wrong spiritual path. We will need to insist on our rights, or we will react by paying back the offender what we think he deserves.

Most often, though, the need to guard our hearts comes as we experience the little annoyances of everyday life. Develop the habit, then, of watching over your soul so that you do not merely excuse a rash temper or cutting words. Do not deceive yourself into thinking these cause no harm. See that you do not hold on to anger long—and take care that you never expect too much from feeble human nature!

If you want to experience the deep love of God in prayer, then, in your everyday life, learn to forgive the way God and Christ forgive—*freely*, to the extent that blood was shed. Take the command literally: ". . . [forgive] each other, just as in Christ God forgave you" (Ephesians 4:32).

May the blood that cleanses our conscience from dead works teach us another great lesson of faith—let this blood cleanse us from *selfishness*, too. The love that the blood of Christ reveals is evidence that a pardoning grace flows to us from God. Let this love take possession of us and flow through us to others, even in their worst fault.

When we are free inwardly to forgive and love other men and women, it is the evidence that we fully know that God has forgiven us. This is the faith I am speaking of when I say we need faith in God's pardoning grace in order to know our prayers are heard and answered.

THE SECRET OF BELIEVING PRAYER

My forgiving Father, sometimes I'm so blind. . . .

I forget that my own sins are crimes of spirit, deserving of death. And I act as if the sins of others are worse than my own.

Open my eyes to the truth that I have been fully forgiven and now I'm free from penalty. Fill me, Father, with your grace so that I can freely cancel the penalties I would exact from others.

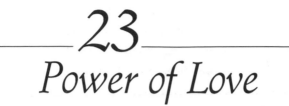

23
Power of Love

Love never fails. . . .

1 Corinthians 13:8

Our daily life out in the world makes up the balance of our true communion with God, and it determines our effectiveness in prayer.

Often, when a Christian comes to pray, he does his best to cultivate a certain "spiritual" frame of mind, which he thinks will please God. If this is true of you, then you have misunderstood, or forgotten, that life does not consist of so many loose pieces. We cannot pick up one piece of our life now and another piece later.

Life is a whole—and God views the pious mind-set we bring as we come to prayer in light of the attitude we hold toward people during our everyday life. . . . The whole tone of my life during the day is what God uses to measure what I am and what I really desire—not the spiritual frame of mind I call up. So I must see that drawing close to God is closely bound up with my relationship to others, and to earth. Failure here will cause failure there. . . .

In our life with people, the one thing on which everything depends is *love*. The spirit of forgiveness is the spirit of love. Because God is love, He forgives. Consequently, it is only as we are dwelling in the love of God that we can forgive as God forgives.

Our love for others is the evidence of our love for God. It is our grounds for confidence before God in prayer. It is our assurance that our prayer will be heard (See 1 John 4:20).

No measure of faith will do, no manner of good works will profit us, if we have no love (See 1 Corinthians 13). It is love that unites with God, and it is love that proves the reality of our faith. . . .

Love is of utmost importance when we labor in prayer for others, and it bears special consequences. We sometimes give ourselves to the work of Christ out of enthusiasm for His cause, or merely for our own spiritual health. And we miss the fact that we must live in the Spirit and image of our Lord, in self-sacrificing love for those whose souls we seek. No wonder that our faith is feeble and fails to conquer.

We must look on each wretched man or woman—no matter how unlovable they might be—in light of the tender love of Jesus, the Shepherd who seeks the lost. We must see Jesus

in this one and, for Jesus' sake, take them up in a
heart that really loves.

This is the secret of believing prayer—prayer
that is fervent and has powerful effect. . . .
Do not forget: A loving life is the condition of
believing prayer. . . . He who gives himself to let
the love of God dwell in him, and makes it a
habit in his daily life to love as God loves, this
one will have the power to believe in the Love
that hears every prayer.

THE SECRET OF BELIEVING PRAYER

*Merciful Father, unfailing in love!—I
want the kind of heart that's merciful and clean . . . a
channel of your love.*

*My Father, show me your unfailing love for
someone today . . . and allow me, as your child, to
help bear them up gently . . . for the sake of your
Name.*

24

The Mystery of Longsuffering

For now we see through a glass, darkly . . .
now I know in part; but then shall I know . . .
And now abideth faith. . . .

1 Corinthians 13:12–13, KJV

Of all the mysteries about prayer, the greatest is why we need to *persevere*. Why is it that the Lord—who is so loving, and who longs to bless us—should have to be asked over and over, sometimes year after year, before the answer comes? This matter of longsuffering in prayer is not easy to understand. And it forms one of our greatest practical difficulties in terms of our prayer life.

When we pray and persevere in prayer, and still the answer does not come, it is so easy for our slothful human nature to stop praying, thinking that God must have some secret reason for withholding the answer. Beware, for this line of reasoning has the appearance of pious submission!

We can only overcome this difficulty in the long battle of prayer by faith. Consider these necessities:

Faith takes its stand upon God's Word.

Faith stands on the name—that is, the nature—of Jesus.

Faith yields itself, not to the fleshly desires and earthly ends we seek in our prayers, but to the leading of the Spirit.

Faith seeks only to see God's will accomplished, and God's honor lifted up in its prayer.

The man or woman who stands on this kind of faith need never be discouraged when the answer is delayed. From Scripture, we know that the power of believing prayer is unstoppable—irresistible in its force. Real faith can *never* be disappointed.

Just as water must be gathered up until a stream can come down with full force and exercise its most irresistible power, so too, there must often be a heaping up of prayer, as it were, until God sees that the measure is full. And then the answer comes with power. . . .

Remember: There may be things around us, or in the great system of being of which we are a small part, or in God's government, things that must be put right through our prayer. And then the answer can fully come. . . .

Everlasting Love burns with the desire to reveal himself fully to His beloved. God will never delay one moment longer than is absolutely necessary.

My Father, there is so often a great battle in me—between wanting my prayer answered right now, and waiting to see your greater purposes fulfilled.

I commit into your hands all the matters that are concerning me—knowing that you are not a cold-hearted general, but a Father who is wise in love.

I will wait, in peace, for your answer.

25
The Bride of Christ

*Paul, an apostle—sent not from men nor by man,
but by Jesus Christ and God the Father . . .
to the churches. . . .*

———

Galatians 1:1–2

Devote yourselves to prayer. . . .

———

Colossians 4:2

Most churches think their members are
gathered into one, simply to care for one another
and to build up one another. They do not know
that God rules the world by the prayers of His
saints—that prayer is the power by which Satan
is conquered, that by prayer the Church on earth
has power and authority over the powers of the
heavenly world.

We do not remember, it seems, that Jesus
promised to set apart every assembly of believers
gathered in His name to be a gateway for heaven
to enter the earth—a holy body of believers

where His presence may be felt and His power seen as the Father fulfills the godly desires of His people.

There *will* be great blessing when God's people meet as one in the name of Jesus—that is, when they meet in order to have His presence in the midst of a body that is all united in the Holy Spirit. When this is so, then a body of believers may boldly claim the promise that whatever they agree to ask shall be done by the Father. . . .

Let us learn this lesson as we pray for the Church of our Lord Christ: She is like a poor widow in the absence of her husband—apparently at the mercy of her enemy and helpless to protect herself or retaliate.

When we pray for the Lord's Church, or for any portion of it that is under the world's power, let us ask Him to visit her with mighty workings of His Spirit. Let us ask Him to prepare her for His coming.

When we pray in this way, we can do so in faith that is full and sure.

THE SECRET OF BELIEVING PRAYER.

My Father, I long for you to come and fill my heart . . . to speak words of hope and faith through me . . . to take hold of my hands and use them to serve.

106

Come, Father, to the center of my being . . . reign over my minutes and my days. Draw me together with others in your family who want to see you fall upon us anew, so that we can wait together, building a fire of hope. . . .

26
God Goes With Us

Jesus said, "Go into all the world. . . ."

Mark 16:15

Jesus said, "[Teach others] everything I have commanded you. And surely I will be with you always, to the very end of the age."

Matthew 28:20

Then the Master said, "Well done, good and faithful servant! You have been faithful with a few things; I will put you in charge of many things. Come and share your master's happiness!"

Matthew 25:23

We know as Christians that our new life is to be one of service and obedience to God. But so often we forget the whole object of the gospel and the glory of our redemption in Christ. With a wrong view of our new life, we will be easily discouraged in our failures and give up.

The gospel shows us that when Christ purchased us for God with His blood, He made possible something that is beyond our thoughts or powers. Jesus revealed God—not as Law-Giver and Judge, exacting from us every bit of punishment—but as a Father. And this Father is one who empowers us by grace, and who deals with each one of us according to our capacity as we learn and grow. And He accepts the devotion and the intention of the heart.

We understand this when it comes to a good earthly father and his child.

Let's say that a child of ten is doing some small chore for this father, or helping him with his work. The work that the child is capable of doing may be very defective—and yet it makes the father smile with joy and gives him hope. Why? Because he sees it as an evidence of the child's love for him, an evidence of obedience and the desire to do well in the father's eyes. The father also sees it as the pledge of what the child's willing spirit will do for him later in life when his intelligence and strength and skill have increased. The child has served the father with a perfect heart—though the perfect heart does not mean that, at the moment, the work is perfect.

In this way, our heavenly Father looks upon our hearts, longing to find a simple childlike attitude in us—a heart that makes deep reverence for God and loving service to Him our one focus.

True, we may be deeply embarrassed and humbled by momentary uprisings of our evil nature. But God's Spirit teaches us to say—not as an excuse but as a cry for more strength in our spirit—"It is not I but sin that dwells in me." . . .

Have you received this witness of the Holy Spirit—that the Father sees and accepts in you a heart that longs to love and obey Him completely?

THE BELIEVER'S SECRET OF A PERFECT HEART

My Father, I am so thankful that I am enfolded in you, because in Christ I am "accepted in the beloved." Here, so close to you, it's less painful to look out at my failings and rebellions and see what a resistant, wicked servant I can be.

Thank you that you don't send me out, away from your presence when you ask me to obey . . . but you go with me . . . so that with each step of obedience I can hear your encouraging word—"Well done."

27
Rise and Walk

*T*hose who hope in the Lord will renew their
strength. They will soar on wings like eagles;
they will run and not grow weary,
they will walk and not be faint.

Isaiah 40:31

*W*hen Jesus saw [the invalid] lying there,
and knew that he already had been in that condition
[for thirty-eight years], he said to him,
"Do you want to be made well?" . . .
[Then] Jesus said to him, "Rise . . . and walk."

John 5:6, 8, NKJV

*T*here are many marks of spiritual health,
and the apostle John points out to us one of
them—*walking*. Jesus said to the sick man, "Rise
and walk," and the man was restored to full
health and vigor, able to take part in all the work
of life.

This is a wonderful picture, suggesting the

kind of spiritual health that God wants to restore to us. . . . It is the Risen One who says to us, "Rise and walk." He gives us the power of resurrected life.

Our new life is a walk *in* Christ: "As ye have . . . received Christ Jesus . . . so walk ye in him" (Colossians 2:6, KJV).

Our new life is a walk *like* Christ: "Whoever claims to live in him must walk as Jesus did" (1 John 2:6). . . .

It is a walk "in the light, as he is in the light" (1 John 1:7). It is a walk of faith—with all its power coming from God and Christ and the Holy Spirit, flowing to the soul that is learning how to turn away from the world and to stop drawing our strength from the power offered by the world. . . .

How wonderful we would find our daily lives to be if we discovered how this spiritual walk is possible—if we actively believed that God sent His Almighty Son and the Holy Spirit to call us and prepare us for an earthly life with heavenly power beyond anything man could dare to imagine or hope for!

When a physician heals a patient, he acts on him from without and tries to bring the patient to a point where he is independent of further medical help. The physician wants to restore the patient to perfect health and then leave him. In both of these things, the work of the Lord Jesus is exactly the opposite: Jesus works from *within*, and

He enters in the power of the Spirit into our very lives—coming to stay and never depart. . . .

Christ's condition for spiritual health and powerful success is to bring us into such dependence upon Him that we shall not be able, for one single moment, to live without Him.

If we want to live in this world, having a life of true spiritual power, we must learn that Christ himself is our life in a sense that so many cannot begin to conceive. The prevailing feeble and sickly Christian life is due entirely to the fact that we do not lay hold of a divine truth:

As long as we continue to expect Christ to do something for us from heaven, in single acts of grace from time to time—and each time, trusting Him only to give us the earthly answer, which lasts only for a little while—then we will never be restored to perfect spiritual health. But if we see, just once, that there is to be nothing of our own for a single moment, if we learn to accept it from Him and trust Him for it, then the life of Christ becomes the health of our soul.

Health is nothing but life in its normal, undisturbed activity. Christ gives us health by giving us himself as our life—and so He becomes our strength for our walk in the spirit.

THE MINISTRY OF INTERCESSORY PRAYER

My Father, I need your Holy Spirit, the wellspring of life to my soul, to flow through me today.

Help me to accomplish the works in spirit that you have for me to do today . . . to speak the simple word of power and hope . . . to lift the weight of someone's heavy spirit.

I want to walk, today, in the path of your Spirit . . . to live and move and have my being in you.

28
Our Stronghold

*Fight the good fight of the faith. Take hold of the
eternal life to which you were called. . . .*

1 Timothy 6:12

*Since the promise of entering [God's] rest still stands,
let us be careful that none of [us] be found to have
fallen short of it . . . the message [we have] heard . . .
[must be combined] with faith . . . [so that] we who
have believed enter that rest. . . .*

Hebrews 4:1–3

*M*any Christians strive all their lives against
the Lord and His callings. Because they are not at
rest but feel an inner conflict, they think that this
is the spiritual warfare of the believer. They are
deceived.

What most Christians wrestle against is this:
They are unwilling to abandon everything and to
surrender themselves to the Lord.

This is not the spiritual battle the Lord wants

115

to lead us into. No, the conflict He wants us to enter does not pitch us into inner turmoil, nor does it need to last for years. The Lord himself desires that we should break through the "enemies" that would hold us back and immediately enter into the fortress of faith that is at rest in God.

There is a second conflict, which endures for life, and Paul calls this "the fight of faith." The chief characteristic of this battle is *faith itself*. He who understands that the principal element in the battle is to believe, and then acts accordingly, will always win the battle. For as Paul says, we must take up "the shield of faith," as this is the only way we may extinguish the flaming darts of anxiety, fear, and unbelief that are fired into our souls by the evil one.

What exactly is the fight of faith? Is it striving to believe that the Lord will come to help me? No, it is not that at all—though many Christians unfortunately think that is the case.

In a war it is of supreme importance that I place myself in a stronghold or fortress that cannot be shaken. In this kind of stronghold, even a weak platoon of soldiers can continue to resist a powerful enemy. We must go in to such an unshakable stronghold—in fact, we *have* gone in, and we *stand* here, strong and secure, if only we would see it!—and as long as we remain hidden here we are invincible.

Our stronghold is Christ. By faith, we stand in

Him. And by faith we know that nothing the enemy fires at us—neither earthly distresses, nor condemning accusations, nor fearful threats shouted at us over the walls of faith—*nothing* can tear down our mighty fortress!

The wiles of Satan are all aimed at one thing: to deceive us into stepping outside of our fortress, and to engage with him in battle on the open plain. For out there—outside of Christ—he always overcomes.

If only we would remember to recognize that every conflict is a spiritual conflict—if only we would remember to strive to win in *faith*. Then we would always win, for then Satan must deal with Christ, who always overcomes. For "this is the victory that has overcome the world—our faith" (1 John 5:4, NKJV).

The reason that our victory is only by faith, and the reason that the "good fight" is the fight of faith is this: Our Lord Jesus purchased the victory with His humility, His death on the cross, and His blood—and so He alone can give power over the enemy. If we have chosen to place our souls *in Christ*—if we stand in Him daily, live and move and have our being in Him alone—then the victory is ours. . . .

In ourselves we can achieve nothing, but in Christ we are more than conquerors. By faith, we stand in Him, righteous before God. And in Him we are strong against our enemies.

THE BELIEVER'S NEW LIFE

My Father, sometimes I have tried to hand my whole life to you. But now I see that, like a soldier learning a discipline, I can train myself to walk in your Spirit by daily and minute-by-minute submitting the events of my life to you.

Whatever comes today, Father—whether it jars and makes me angry, whether it tempts me or calls me to truer obedience—I will hand it back to you.

You are my stronghold, and in you I will not be thrown down.

29
The Promised Spirit

[God] redeemed us
in order that the blessing given to Abraham
might come to the Gentiles through Christ Jesus,
so that by faith we might receive
the promise of the Spirit.

———

Galatians 3:14

Follow the way of love
and eagerly desire spiritual gifts . . .
I will pray with my spirit . . .
I will sing with my spirit . . .
[praise] God with your spirit. . . .

———

1 Corinthians 14:1, 15–16

*T*he apostles were men who had accepted, in faith, Jesus' promise of the Spirit.

On the night before the crucifixion, Christ had spoken to them more than once about the Holy

119

Spirit. And when He was ready to ascend into heaven, He said to them again, "You shall be baptized with the Holy Spirit not many days from now" (Acts 1:5, NKJV).

If you had asked any one of the disciples before the day of Pentecost what this promise meant, I am sure he could not have told you. These men had no idea what was to come.

What they did do, apparently, was to take the word of Jesus, and if they had occasion to talk— more likely, to argue—about this promise, I believe they must have said: "He did such wonderful things for us while He was on earth. Now that He is in glory He can do things that are infinitely more wonderful." Perhaps they waited in that kind of awed expectancy.

You and I must also accept Jesus' promise by faith. We must say, "The promise of the filling of the Holy Spirit is for *me*. I accept it at the hand of Jesus himself."

True, you may not understand what it will mean. You may not feel it as you would like to feel it. In fact, you may feel weak and sinful and far away from God. But still you may say—you have a *right* to say—the promise of the Holy Spirit is for *me*. Are you ready to say that?

Are you ready, in faith, to trust the promise and the word and the love of Jesus?

I know there are many believers who struggle to find out where they are lacking. They have given their lives to Jesus, wanting with all their heart to serve Him. They love Him, and they have even sought to humble themselves on their faces in prayer. The only problem is that they have not learned simply to say: He has promised me the Holy Spirit, and He will do it.

I tell you this so that you can be filled with the holy courage to believe: When you get a promise from God, it is worth just as much as the fulfillment. A promise brings you into direct contact with the heart and mind and will of God for you.

Honor God, then, by trusting the promise and obeying Him. If there is any preparation that needs to occur within you, never fear—God knows about it. And if there is any light of spiritual understanding that needs to be opened up to you—He himself will show you. All that you need to do is to count on Him to do it.

Trust the promise—trust the One who promises!—and say, "The fullness of the Holy Spirit is meant for me."

THE BELIEVER'S ABSOLUTE SURRENDER

My Father, I have experienced moments, sometimes days, of your grace and presence. But I want to live more fully in you . . . have you more fully in me.

Fill me now, Father. Drive the darkness from the corners within. I want to know the fiery brightness of your heart and mind and will for me . . . to be empowered to act and speak as you guide me.

30
The War of Spirit and Flesh

*Jesus prayed: "I have revealed you, [Father], to those
whom you gave me out of the world. . . . I will
remain in the world no longer, but they are still in the
world, and I am coming to you. Holy Father, protect
them by the power of your name. . . . I have given
them your word and the world has hated them, for
they are not of the world any more than I am of the
world. . . . [Set them apart for your use, and make
them holy] by the truth; your word is truth."*

John 17:6, 11, 14, 16–17, NIV

When Jesus promised to send us the
Comforter, He referred to the Holy Spirit as the
one "whom the world cannot receive."

You must see this: The spirit of this world is
devotion to the visible, and it is in irreconcilable
antagonism with the Spirit of Jesus in heaven,
where God and His will are everything.

The world has rejected the Lord Jesus and, no

matter what spiritual disguises this spirit puts on, it is still the same untameable foe.

It was to draw this distinction that Jesus said of His true disciples—in fact, to indicate one clear mark of a disciple: "They are not of the world, even as I am not of it" (John 17:16). Likewise, Paul said, "We have not received the spirit of the world but the Spirit who is from God" (1 Corinthians 2:12).

Make no mistake, the spirit of this world and the Spirit of God are engaged in a life-and-death conflict with each other. That is why God has always called on His people to separate themselves from the world and to live as pilgrims whose treasure and whose heart are in heaven.

Is that what we see in our own lives?

Isn't it more true to say that, once we reach a place in our walk as Christians where we have tamed most of the obvious sins, once we have comforted ourselves with the assurance of heaven, that we decide we are as free to enjoy the world as fully as others? We live in a way that there is little to be seen of true spirituality in our conversation, our everyday walk, in our character and commitment. And could we expect anything else when we do not seek or enjoy the fullness of the Spirit that is promised to us?

Nothing but light can drive out darkness. Nothing but the Spirit from heaven can expel the spirit of this world. When a man or woman does not surrender to God, to be filled with the Spirit of Jesus and the Spirit of heaven, they must remain under the power of the spirit of this world.

I hear a piercing cry that rises from the whole Church of our Lord Christ: "Who will save us from the power of the spirit of this world?"

Let your answer be: "Nothing can save me, no one can save me—except the Spirit of God!

"I must be filled with the Spirit!"

THE BELIEVER'S FULL BLESSING OF PENTECOST

My Father, I want your Spirit to take the battlefield today. I want devotion to you to be the banner that flies above my words and actions today.

Father, turn your Light upon my inner man right now and expose the secret devotion I hold . . . to my own opinion . . . to reputation . . . to material things . . . to positions of power that I envy.

Win the battle in me, so that my heart can be cleared and prepared for you, as King, to save others who are falling in the fight.

31
Vessels of Glory

Jesus said, "I pray . . . for those you have given me,
for they are yours. All I have is yours, and all you
have is mine. And glory will come to me through
them. . . . I have given them the glory
that you gave me. . . ."

John 17:9–10, 22

Jesus said, "By myself I can do nothing . . .
for I seek not to please myself
but him who sent me. . . .
I have come down from heaven not to do my will
but to do the will of him who sent me."

John 5:30; 6:38

*M*an was created to be a vessel into which
God could pour His wisdom, goodness, beauty,
and power. That is the heritage of the believer.

It is God who makes the cherubim and
seraphim flames of fire. The unrestricted glory of
God passes through them. They are vessels

prepared by God, sent from God, that they might let God's glory shine through them.

And so it was with the Son. Sin came in—the terrible sin, first, of the fallen angels, and then the sin of man. They exalted themselves against God and refused to receive the glory of God into themselves because they were seeking their own glory, and so they fell into outer darkness—first the devils, and then man. But Christ came to restore us.

And so He lived among us, day by day, and depended upon the Father for everything. Notice that, during His temptation in the wilderness, He would not touch a bit of bread until the Father gave it to Him. Although He was very hungry and had the power to turn a stone into bread, He would not eat until the Father sent ministering angels.

It is by this life of absolute dependence upon God that the glorified Christ will one day fulfill the great plan—that God shall be *all in all* (1 Corinthians 15:28). . . .

Christ did *all* in obedience. What is obedience? It is simply surrendering my will in order to act in accordance with the will of another.

When a soldier obeys the orders of a commander, or when a student obeys the instructions of an instructor, he sets aside his own will. *My will is my life.* When I obey, I give myself to the rule and mastery of another—and that is what Christ did. . . .

Learn from Christ that the beauty and purpose of having life is so that you can surrender it to God—for that is when God can fill you with His glory.

THE BELIEVER'S ABSOLUTE SURRENDER

My Father, I will seek you today for more than supplies of peace and strength, healing and provision.

I hand you my will now, and ask that you keep me alert to the people and circumstances you send into my life today . . . alert to do your will in all things.

32
Witnesses

Jesus said, ". . . you will receive power when the Holy Spirit comes on you; and you will be my witnesses . . . to the ends of the earth."

Acts 1:8

*T*hese were the very last words of our Lord before His ascension. They linked the promise of the Spirit with the ends of the earth.

From this, we must see that the fullness of the Spirit will be given only in connection with our open willingness to see the kingdom of God extended. And the power for carrying the gospel to people, whether those near to us or far away, is absolutely dependent on the measure of the Spirit's presence with us. Every time we pray for the power of the Spirit, our goal should be this: to testify of Jesus with our lives as well as our words. . . .

Prayer is conflict with the powers of darkness. And it is fellowship with the cross of Christ and its intercession. In prayer, we stir up our strength to take hold of God and to prevail with Him in bringing His blessing down on the men and women around us.

When we grow into this consciousness during prayer—"I have power with God; He will listen to me; He will give an answer"—then our life's mission will become more than ever a triumph of the cross. We will find its power at work in our own life, before the throne of heaven, and here on the battlefield for those who are lost.

Test your own devotional life by the influence it really exercises in fulfilling the mystery of Christ in the world. Believe, when you are praying in secret, that your work here will count for eternity—and believe that you are receiving real power that will make itself felt in whatever sphere God has positioned you for establishing His kingdom on earth.

THE BELIEVER'S CALL TO COMMITMENT

My Father, fill me with the hope and joy of your presence today . . . and give me words of truth, seasoned with grace, when others ask about the hope that's in me.

I ask that your presence—gentle, humble, brilliant—grow so strong in me that my very life will be an intercession, where you can demonstrate yourself in this world.

33
Sword of the Spirit

*Take . . . the sword of the Spirit, which is
the word of God.*

Ephesians 6:17

*T*he Holy Spirit is the mighty power of God.
The Spirit-filled Christian is to be strengthened
and equipped for God's service, and for the
spiritual warfare that comes when we try to enter
God's kingdom, or when we try to see it
established in any way here on earth.

Paul warns us that "our struggle is not against
flesh and blood, but against the rulers, against
the authorities, against the powers of this dark
world and against the spiritual forces of evil in
the heavenly realms" (Ephesians 6:12). It is crucial
for us to live every day clothed in the whole
armor of God—which means standing strong in
Christ and in the strength of His might. . . .

When Paul says, "Put on the full armor of
God" (vv. 11 and 13) . . . he mentions only one
offensive weapon—the sword of the Spirit, which
is the Word of God.

To know the power of God's Word and how to use it effectively, we need only look to our Leader, the Captain of the Lord's host. When Jesus met Satan in the wilderness, He conquered the evil one by the Word of God alone. He had studied that word, loved it, obeyed it, and lived in it. So the Holy Spirit found within Him the familiar words with which He could meet and conquer every satanic suggestion.

To lift the sword of the Spirit in the moment of battle means that I have lived in the Word and have it living in me—that I have lived it out, and it has mastered my person. Only the Spirit of Christ within me enables the power of my faith to cast away Satan by the Word of God. . . .

Whether I am locked in a struggle with worldliness, or with open or hidden sin, with weak faith or dark superstition, with nominal Christianity or a backsliding church—or with the kingdom of darkness itself—the Word of God will always be my weapon of victory if I know how to use it correctly. . . .

To prepare you for this warfare, Christ must be revealed to you, inwardly, calling you to turn away from every sin—above all, the sin of unbelief. He must first war against *you* and the evil that is in you with the sharp two-edged sword that proceeds from His mouth against all your unrighteousness (Revelation 2:16).

I tell you, yield your inmost soul to the sword of truth that proceeds from the mouth of Jesus—

so that your secret intentions and inclinations are revealed in the light of God and His holiness. Only then will you have faith and strength to wield the Word of God against every enemy. . . .

Let us listen to the heavenly declaration that calls us to the war. Confess and repent for having so seldom stood in the strength of the Lord and the power of His might. . . .

Remember, it is in your own life that you must prove the power of God's Word in prayer and intercession, bringing your soul to surrender and cleansing. I say again, it is in your own soul that you must learn to use the sword of the Spirit— and then your new love for the Lord and for other captive souls will awaken you to the war.

May the Word of God, taken into the center of your soul, become in reality the sword of the Spirit. Then you will carry it as if firmly strapped to your thigh, so that you are always ready to meet the enemy and to set his captives free.

THE BELIEVER'S CALL TO COMMITMENT

My Father, I know that in your hands the sword of the Spirit is as delicate and restoring as a surgeon's scalpel. Reveal to me today cancers that you want to excise from my soul.

Prepare me, Father. Make me healthy in soul . . . so that in love . . . in your fathomless love . . . I may speak clean-cutting words of truth that do not harm but set free other sick and dying captives.

133

34
Our Commission

*Y*ou *were like sheep going astray, but now you have*
returned to [Jesus,] the Shepherd and Overseer of
your souls.

1 Peter 2:25

*F*or God *was pleased to have all his fullness dwell in*
[Jesus], and through him to reconcile to himself
all things. . . .

Colossians 1:19–20

*J*esus said, *". . . As the Father has sent me, I am*
sending you."

John 20:21

*T*he heart of Christ is set on claiming His
rightful dominion over the world that He has
redeemed and won for himself. And He counts
on us, His disciples, to undertake and carry out
the work. . . . We are the advance-guard of His
conquering hosts. . . .

Christ does not teach or argue, ask or plead: He simply commands. "Go and make disciples of all nations" (Matthew 28:19). . . . He has attached us to himself in a love that makes us want to obey. He has breathed His own resurrection Spirit into us, and He can count on us. . . .

The command is not for others, it is for me—for every one of us. In the Church, there is no "privileged class" that can rest comfortably in an honored position while some special "lower class of servants" bears all the weight of duty to Christ. It is not left to specially called "missionaries" or "evangelists" to carry the gospel to every creature.

The life Christ gives to every one of us is His own life—the Spirit He breathes upon us is His very own Spirit. And the one attitude He will work into every one of us is an attitude of self-sacrificing love. The very nature of our salvation—if it is true salvation—is to bring every one of us into full and healthy access to Jesus Christ. And if we are becoming one with Him, then we will feel the urge to give out what we have received.

Now you must understand something: The *command* is, in the truest sense, no command at all—not some arbitrary law that is laid upon us. It is a truth that must dawn upon us from within—a spiritual law that waits to be discovered, so that you say, "Yes! I see the wonderful truth of it!"

What is that truth?

We are His body. We now occupy His place on earth. His will and His love long to carry out the work He began—*through us*. And now, in place of Jesus himself, as true sons of God, we find the glory of God the Father dawning in us as we live our lives in order to win a lost world back to Him. . . .

Accept His command.

Place yourself entirely at His good disposal, to do His wonderful will.

Begin, this minute, to live in His kingdom.

THE BELIEVER'S SECRET OF OBEDIENCE

My Father, thank you for reminding me that you sent your Son to win us . . . not to a set of doctrines or beliefs . . . not to conform us to a standard of outward words or actions . . . but to win us to you.

I surrender my home, everything I own, my goals and aspirations, the work of my hands . . . all of it to your service.

I accept your command. . . . I am at your service. . . . Perform your will in me, through me, today.

35
High and Holy Destiny

Holy brothers, who share in the heavenly calling, fix your thoughts on Jesus. . . . See to it . . . that none of you has a sinful, unbelieving heart. . . . Let us then approach the throne of grace with confidence, so that we may receive mercy and find grace to help. . . .

Hebrews 3:1, 12; 4:16

*I*n the study of the starry heavens, much depends upon us having a clear understanding of the relative sizes and magnitudes of the shining bodies we are viewing. We need some sense of the size of each star and planet—and a sense of the infinite regions of space in which they move—or there can be no true knowledge of the cosmos and its relation to this earth.

There is a parallel here with the spiritual heavens—that is, the invisible realm—and the heavenly life to which we are called. We need to gain some sense of this other realm, its reality and vastness and power, if we are to understand the truth about a life of intercession. For intercessory prayer is nothing more or less than a wonderful interaction between heaven and earth—and everything depends on us gaining a right understanding of magnitudes—that is, the relative importance of things—in the spiritual realm.

Let us consider the "magnitudes" of three forces that interact, in terms of the spiritual realm:

There is the world, with its great needs. The world is entirely dependent upon, and waiting to be helped, by intercession.

There is God in heaven, with His all-sufficient supply for all those needs, waiting to be asked.

There is a Church—of which, you and I are a part—with its magnificent calling and its sure promises, waiting to be roused to a sense of its awesome responsibility and power.

God seeks intercessors. . . .

If God so loves the world, if He so longs to bless—then there must be some reason for His holding back. What can it be?

Scripture says it is because of our "unbelief"— because of our *faithlessness* and, consequently, our *unfaithfulness* as God's people. He has taken us into partnership with himself. He has honored us, and He has bound himself in the matter of bringing light and blessing from the heavenly realm into this earthly realm of darkness. How is that so? Because He has made our prayers the standard against which He measures out the working of His power.

Lack of intercession is one of the chief causes of the lack of blessing we see.

If only we would turn our eyes and hearts away from everything in this world—the weak things of this world we so readily look to when we are in need. If only we would fix the eyes of our faith upon this God who hears prayer—fix them upon Him, until the magnificence of His promises and His power and His loving purposes overwhelm us! Then our whole heart, our whole life, would be transformed into one great intercession.

For this to happen, there is another "magnitude" to which our eyes must be opened. That is the stupendous privilege and power of intercessors.

Among us, as Christians, there is a false humility, which makes a great virtue out of saying things like, "Oh, I'm not a very good Christian really. My faith is so small, and God doesn't answer my poor feeble prayers." The fact is, people who say such things have never really seen their utter nothingness and they are, most often, secretly hoping someone will object and tell them how wonderful and loved by God they really are.

If we truly realize our utter *nothingness*—when comparing our puny "powers" to God's vast eternal power—then we will never apologize for our feebleness at all. On the contrary we will glory in our utter weakness, knowing that this is the one condition that makes it possible for Christ's power to rest upon us! We would judge our own power and influence before God in prayer, as little by what we see and feel, as we judge the size and strength of the sun or stars by what the eye can see.

Faith sees itself as man created in the image and likeness of God, to be God's representative in this world to have dominion over it. Faith sees itself as man redeemed and lifted into union with Christ, drawing our life from Him, identified with Him, and clothed with His power in intercession.

Faith sees the intercession of the saints as it truly is—as part of the life of the Holy Trinity, in which the believer as God's child asks favor and blessing from the Father, through the Son, through the Spirit.

Faith sees something of the divine fitness, the divine beauty, of this scheme for making salvation come to the earth through the means of intercession. And faith awakens our souls to an awareness of our amazing and wonderful destiny.

THE MINISTRY OF INTERCESSORY PRAYER

My Father, thank you for sending Jesus, a faithful Light, to lead me through spiritual darkness to you.

I commit myself to learn faithfulness . . . and self-sacrifice . . . and obedience . . . so that I can begin to pray with the force of heaven . . . to release others from spiritual prisons . . . where they are lost, confused, clinging to earthly securities that are failing.

36
Set Apart

*While they were worshiping the Lord and fasting,
the Holy Spirit said, "Set apart for me Barnabas and
Saul for the work to which I have called them."*

———

Acts 13:2

*If a man cleanses himself from [selfish and evil
purposes], he will be an instrument for noble
purposes, [set apart as] holy, useful to the Master and
prepared to do any good work.*

———

2 Timothy 2:21

If we, as Christians, are going to take part in
the work of God as He establishes His kingdom
on earth—more importantly, if God is to bless
our work—then we must stand in right relation
to the Holy Spirit. . . .

No doubt, many of us often cry to God for the
Holy Spirit to come upon us as a Spirit of power,
and when we feel a measure of power, we thank
God for it. But God desires something more,

something higher: God wants us to seek for the Holy Spirit as a Spirit of power in our own heart and life—to conquer self, to cast out sin, and to work into us the blessed and beautiful image of Jesus.

There is a difference between the power of the Spirit as a gift and the power of the Spirit for the grace of a holy life. A man or woman may have a measure of the power of the Holy Spirit, but if the Spirit does not rule their heart as the Spirit of grace and holiness, this defect—and it is a defect—will be seen, sooner or later, in the things they do and say, and in their work for God. A person may be effective in leading someone else to Christ, for example, but without this deeper grace of the Holy Spirit he will never be able to help people on to find a higher standard of spiritual life. . . .

A man or woman who is separated in heart to the Holy Spirit is one who says, "Father, let the Holy Spirit have full dominion over me—in my home, in my attitudes, in every word that comes from my mouth, in every thought of my heart, in every feeling toward others. Let your Holy Spirit have full possession of me."

Has that been the desire of your heart? Is it the spiritual covenant you want to make with God—to be a man or woman separated in heart and given over to the Holy Spirit's use?

May God grant that the Holy Spirit's call— "separate [set apart] for me"—will enter into the inmost place of your being. May it search you, and if God shows you that self-life, self-will, and self-exaltation are there, then humble yourself before Him.

Make this your aim: to fully separate yourself in heart from the world.

THE BELIEVER'S ABSOLUTE SURRENDER

My Father, I do want my heart to be set apart for you . . . so caught up in the knowledge that you are the only One who has the words and the way of Life . . . that I trust in nothing else but you.

I want to be so sure in this knowledge that I can accept your challenge . . . your assignment . . . to walk closely, lovingly, and clear of judgment . . . beside someone else who is just now looking for the path of Life.

37
Standing

It is we who . . . worship by the Spirit of God, who glory in Christ Jesus, and who put no confidence in the flesh. . . .

Philippians 3:3

Now this is the confidence that we have in Him, that if we ask anything according to His will, He hears us. And if we know that He hears us, whatever we ask, we know that we have the petitions that we asked of him.

1 John 5:14–15, NKJV

In [Christ Jesus] and through faith in him we may approach God with freedom and confidence.

Ephesians 3:12

In his great letter to the Colossians, Paul returns several times to point our attention to God's almighty power.

In the first chapter, he speaks of the Spirit's enlightenment, which shows us that we need the power that raised Christ from the dead to work in us every moment and in every action of our spiritual life (Colossians 1:10–12).

Then he goes much further, and he prays that the exceeding greatness of God's power—that is, the "glorious riches of this mystery, which is Christ in you"—may be made known to us (v. 27). He says that it is this mighty power by which the Spirit strengthens us in our inner man.

Do we have the least idea what this means?

It can only mean one thing: God wants our whole spiritual life to be enlivened, empowered— permanently brought to life—so that the indwelling of Christ in our heart will become a wonderful reality to us.

The Church has nearly lost the thought that the indwelling Christ can be a personal, conscious, and continuous experience. And before you or I can find this marvelous reality in our faith and experience, we must learn to be confident that the exceeding greatness of God's power is a part of the inheritance of every Christian. And the Holy Spirit is the "down payment." . . .

There are other attributes of God—His love, His righteousness, His holiness—for which we bless His name. But we need to be reminded, over and over, that His power is our one true confidence. It is an almighty power, unstoppable, and by this power He can complete all that He means to do in us, and all the purposes that He has set for our lives.

Let us worship and adore, until every thought . . . is summed up in one statement of faith:

"[He] is able to do immeasurably more than all we ask or imagine, according to his power that is at work within us!" (Ephesians 3:20).

THE BELIEVER'S CALL TO COMMITMENT

My Father, in you alone do I place my confidence today.

Confident—because you welcome me before your mighty throne—because you promise to stay with me . . . in me.

Confident—because you can speak and make me quick to hear . . . happy to obey.

Confident—because I open my heart to you . . . and your power to work through me is unstoppable.

38
God's Kingdom in Sight

Jesus said, ". . . the righteous will shine like the sun in the kingdom of their Father. He who has ears, let him hear."

———

Matthew 13:43

Suppose someone had asked Jesus of Nazareth, "What is God's purpose in giving you a body—what is your body's highest use?"

He would have said, "The use and the glory of my body is that I can give it as a sacrifice to God. That is my highest purpose."

We might well ask ourselves: What is the highest use of your mind, of your money, of having children?

I pray that God may give you such a glimpse of His kingdom and His glory that every other goal of your life may disappear in its beauty. Then, if you had ten thousand lives, you would say, "This is the beauty and the worth of life, that

God may be all in all to me—that I may prove by all that I am and all I own that God is more than everything, and that life is worth living only as it is given to God to fill it."

Have you yet seen the glory and beauty of God? Are you ready to "sacrifice" everything in order to be able to live daily in His kingdom and for His glory?

Make it your highest joy to begin every day of the rest of your life by praying: "My Father, I give myself up to you entirely. Fill my life with yourself—be my all in all."

You may balk and say, "Isn't that fairly idealistic? Will I be able to live up to such a high goal?"

You will, and this is how you can achieve the highest purposes for your life: Let the Holy Spirit burn in you as a fire with unutterable groanings, crying out to God, asking Him to reveal His presence and His will in you.

Paul tells us that the whole creation is groaning for the redemption of the children of God—and this redemption begins when our spiritually blind eyes are open to the glorious freedom that is ours in Christ (Romans 8). I am persuaded this is what Paul meant when he spoke of the unutterable groanings of the Holy Spirit—that the Spirit aches with longing for the time of glory that is to come, when the kingdom of God will be revealed in us. . . .

My brothers and sisters in Christ, I appeal to

you: Give up your time, your interests—sacrifice your heart's best powers in praying and calling out to God—that He may shine through you as your all in all.

The Believer's Secret of the Master's Indwelling

My Father, *this is my prayer of commitment . . . and I pray this, trusting you to be faithful to all that I commit:*

Prove yourself through all that I am, all that I have, all that I do . . . my goals, my work, my possessions . . . all of it is empty apart from you. Fill me, and continue to fill me, so that the sum of my days here on earth is not vanity.

Keep close to me . . . nudge me back into this path of Life when I begin to wander.

39
Our Crowning Goal

The reverent and worshipful fear of the Lord brings instruction in Wisdom, and humility comes before honor.

———

Proverbs 15:33, Amplified

Clothe yourselves with humility toward one another, because, "God opposes the proud but gives grace to the humble."

———

1 Peter 5:5; Proverbs 3:34

*J*ust yesterday someone asked me, "How can I ever conquer my *pride*?"

The answer is simple. Two things are needed.

First, do the work that God has given you to do: Humble yourself.

Then, trust Him to do the work that is His to do: He will lift you up. . . .

It is *not* your work to struggle and fight, trying

to cast pride out of your nature, and to somehow form within yourself the lowliness of the Holy One—Jesus. No, this is God's work, the very essence of His exaltation. His work is nothing less than to lift you up into the real likeness of His beloved Son.

Your highest work is to take every opportunity to humble yourself before God and man. In faith, believe that God's empowering grace is already at work in you—and believe that more empowering grace will be yours when the toughest challenges come, for they will come.

Draw upon that grace every time your holy conscience shines its flashes, revealing the dark pockets of pride hidden within your heart. Yes, there will be times of failure and falling, but you must stand firm, persistent as a soldier under an unchanging command: *Humble yourself.*

And still you may ask—"What does it mean to humble yourself?" For the spirit of this world has likely planted in your mind many false and sickly notions of what humility is and what it looks like. Very plainly, I will tell you.

To humble yourself, you must do this: Accept with gratitude everything that God allows to come into your life. I mean all things—whether from the world without, or attacks from within; whether from friend or enemy; in nature or in grace. You must change your view of the people and events that come into your life, so that *all things* remind you of your need for humbling, and all things become the means to help you achieve it. To live in humility means that you cease from striving in life under your own weak powers, for your own ends and your own glory, and to receive your life and the power to live it directly from the hand of God.

You must count this kind of humility as the mother-virtue of all others—of love, joy, peace, patience, kindness, goodness, longsuffering, and the rest. Humility is your very first duty before God, the one constant and reliable safeguard that will keep your soul within the kingdom of God.

Each day, set your heart upon living in humility, and you will find that—though it first appears to your flesh to be the dark way, where you will be lost and forgotten—in fact, it is the way of light and all blessing. . . .

Happy is the man or woman who learns to put all hope in God, who stands firm, notwithstanding all the power of pride and self that lies within. . . .

We know the law of human nature: Acts produce habits, habits produce attitudes, attitudes form the will, and the will that is shaped into a right spirit is good character. Though grace is an inward act of God, it requires our cooperation from without. . . .

Remember that water always fills the lowest places first. The "lower," or emptier, a person lies before God, the faster and fuller the in-flow of God's divine character will come.

Remember, too, that the exaltation God promises is not some external glory, like the puny glories offered by the world. All that He has to give us, all that He can give us, is more of himself. . . .

HUMILITY

My Father, I have often been afraid of letting you take full control of my life . . . fearing that it would be all loss . . . sacrifice . . . obedient drudgery.

But now I thank you for the lighted path on which your Spirit leads me . . . where I can see that insisting on my own way bogs me down . . . a fool, stuck in gathering blackness.

Today, Father, I ask that your Spirit, like a laser of light, lead me in all the ways I can turn from my own way . . . to walk in your way of Life.

40
Like Christ

The end will come, when [Christ] hands over the kingdom to God the Father after he has destroyed all dominion, authority and power. For he must reign until he has put all enemies under his feet. . . . When [Christ] has done this, then the Son himself will be made subject to [the Father] who put everything under him, so that God may be all in all.

1 Corinthians 15:24–25, 28

What a great mystery there is in this passage of Scripture. . . .

There is coming a time when the Son of Man himself will be subjected to the Father and will give the kingdom into the Father's hands—and God will be all in all. I cannot begin to understand this mystery; it goes beyond our ability to comprehend.

But I can worship Christ—that is, I can fix my eyes on His life and death and resurrection—and I can bow myself to the will of the Father, just as Christ subjected His life to God. . . .

The whole aim of Christ's coming, the whole aim of our redemption, and the whole aim of Christ's work in our hearts now by the Holy Spirit, is summed up in this: "that God may be all in all."

We need to take this thought into the world with us every day—to keep it in our hearts as a life motto. If we fail to see that this is Christ's goal, then we will never understand the heart attitude that He wants to work into us.

Realize this, take it as fact, make it the aim of your life—to subordinate everything to God. Then we will have a mighty spiritual weapon on our side—that is, the same principle that ruled the life of Christ.

Let your heart and soul and mind be fixed on reaching this one invincible goal, every day for the rest of your life: to be like Christ, clothing yourselves with His lowly attitude. . . .

Have in your heart just one hope and one song—that God may become your all in all!

THE BELIEVER'S ABSOLUTE SURRENDER

My Father, today I ask again that you make my life a weapon in your good and mighty hand. Show me . . . strike from me . . . the thing that keeps me from obeying you.

I ask you to keep my spiritual sight unclouded by self-will. Help me to see that I am sent by you . . . a

*warrior and a servant in spirit . . . to live free and to
free those you will send me to.*

*Let my life, today and every day, prove that you are
God . . . and your hand is mighty over all!*

DAVID HAZARD developed the REKINDLING THE INNER FIRE devotional series to encourage others to keep the "heart" of their faith alive and afire with love for God. He also feels a special need to help Christians of today to "meet" men and women of the past whose experience of God belongs to the whole Church, for all the ages.

Hazard is an award-winning writer, the author of books for both adults and children, with international bestsellers among his many titles. He lives in northern Virginia with his wife, MaryLynne, and three children: Aaron, Joel, and Sarah Beth.